The A - Z
of Betws-y-coed

'Two things are characteristic of this age, and more particularly of this island: the conscious appreciation of natural beauty, and the rapidity with which natural beauty is being destroyed. . .Like the Universe, like life, natural beauty also is a mystery. But whatever it may be, whether casual in its origin, as some hold who love it well, or whether as others hold, such splendour can be nothing less than the purposeful message of God — whatever its interpretation may be, natural beauty is the ultimate spiritual appeal of the Universe, of nature, or of the God of nature, to their nursling man.'

G. M. TREVELYAN

in the Rickman Godlee Lecture for 1931.

The A-Z
of
Betws-y-coed

A miscellany of selected past and present facts associated with the village and parish, including character anecdotes.

by

Donald Lymburn Shaw.

GWASG CARREG GWALCH

Rhif Rhyngwladol/*ISBN*: 0-86381-153-1

Lluniau/*Photographs:* Wyn E. Jones, Donald Shaw

Argraffwyd a chyhoeddwyd gyntaf
yn 1990 gan:
First published in 1990 by:

GWASG CARREG GWALCH
Capel Garmon
Llanrwst
Gwynedd, Cymru (Wales).
☎: 06902 261

CONTENTS

5

FOREWORD

BETWS-Y-COED — THE EMERGING YEARS

An extract from *A Guide to the Vale of Conwy* (1884) by Ellis o'r Nant, quotes an old writer as saying "Ni ddaethom yrŵan i Fetws, hynny ydyw, lle cynnes tymhoraidd" — which translated means, "We came now to Betws, that is, a warm, comfortable place".

And without a doubt the old writer was correct in his assertion, for Betws is a warm and comfortable place, and by the addition of "y coed" (the wood) becomes sheltered too.

Betws-y-coed (Prayer-house in the woods) was at one time a scattered community around an ancient packhorse track with most of its habitations located along the hillsides. These dwellings, called "tyddyn" or small crofts in the cottage style, each had its own small area of pasture wrested from surrounding woodland. So dense were the trees within the locality in Mediaeval times that a squirrel could travel from Dolgarrog some eight miles to the north of the village to Dolwyddelan six miles to the south, without coming to ground.

There is a reference to a forest of Snowdon in the 16th century, and within its boundaries the hillsides within the parish of Betws-y-coed would have been included. In 1639, Cromwell's Book of Survey of all forests beyond Trent refers to Snowdon forest, and confirms it always had laws, courts and a Justice.

All through the centuries Betws-y-coed had this association with woodland and today many properties within the village still claim reference to it — Coed Derw (Oak wood); Ty'n-y-Coed (House in the wood); Coed-y-Celyn (Wood of Holly); Coedmawr (Big Wood); Coedcynhelier (The Hidden Wood).

These dense forests growing on steep hillsides and among protruding crags presented a wild, forbidding and gloomy backcloth to the early residents of Betws-y-coed, and to travelling chroniclers. Leland (*Itinerary in Wales, 1536-39*) writes of dense and trackless woodland and claimed that the, "best wood in Caernarfonshire (now Gwynedd) is by Glinne Kledder (Glyn Lledr) and Capel Kiryk (Capel Curig). Pennant (Travels in Wales 1773 and 1776) considered that the noblest oak in all Wales grew on the western hillsides of the Conwy valley between Betws-y-coed and Gwydir Castle. Edmund Hyde Hall (Description of Caernarvonshire 1809-11) wrote, "from above Capel Curig to Gwydir Castle is thriving woodland", and Hemingway (Panorama of N. Wales 1835) refers to the scenery beyond Pont-y-pair as, "fringed with woods".

These observations by writers of repute were evidence enough of the countryside character from which Betws-y-coed emerged and grew. Much of the ancient forest disappeared to supply fuel for the smelters' furnaces, and tracts of lowland forest were laid waste during the Wars of the Roses. Ceaselessly, clearings were made to establish small agricultural holdings on the lower hillslopes wherever practicable.

Prior to 1758 all the parishes within Nant Conwy were obliged to import potatoes, but as clearance of the woodland and scrub on the hillsides increased more land became available for cultivation and by 1780, 13,200 bushels of potatoes were exported from the port of Conwy.

The hamlet was isolated for the most part and the neighbourhood served only by rough tracks and stony paths through the forested hillsides. Only one partly made-up road was recognised as a 'major' thoroughfare and that was Ffordd Elen (Roman road), but only short sections of the route were followed.

The changes in the forested countryside around Betws-y-coed became more dramatic after 1800 when small farmsteads were finally wrested from the inhospitable rocky hillsides and became permanent clearings. Travel before this year had been arduous and slow, confined to narrow paths through long distances of woodland. In 1800, under the authority of an Act, the old packhorse track (now the B5106) between Betws-y-coed and Llanrwst, via Gwydir Castle, was greatly improved.

While N. Wales had very little surplus for export before the days of the Industrial Revolution, the main exception had

The Royal Oak Hotel in days gone by

been herds of store cattle. As in other parishes, on the uplands above Betws-y-coed and in open grazings in the midst of forest, these cattle were raised successfully and became a prime source of local revenue. Dealers and drovers purchased them at fairs and drove them eastwards at a rate of about twenty miles a day, taking six to eight weeks to arrive in the London markets.

After eleven years under construction a road from Bangor reached Betws-y-coed and several years later, in 1808, the first Irish Mail coach proceeded through the village. By 1815 — the year of Waterloo — the road through the village had achieved the status of a main thoroughfare from London to Holyhead.

When the mail coaches were first introduced turnpike maintenance relied on toll receipts and the necessary labour was supplied by people residing in the area through which roads passed. Heavy mail coaches greatly increased the wear on road surfaces, but were exempt from paying tolls. The demand from Post Office surveyors for further improvement to the Holyhead road met with bitter resistance in the poorer rural areas like Betws-y-coed through which it passed.

THE UNFOLDING YEARS

As travelling conditions improved and expanded, visitors arrived in numbers to explore the vicinity and sample the quality of village hospitality. Betws-y-coed had limited accommodation at the beginning of this period but, as time passed, the numbers of hotels and guest houses increased and the village began to gain a reputation as a peaceful mountain resort and tourist location.

It grew in stature when the Victorian artists, writers and diarists came to the village, admired its situation and climate; the generous hospitality and comfort of the accommodation; the mixed woodland backcloth along the craggy hillsides; and the whitewaved waters of its rivers as they contributed turbulent motion and onrushing voice to the rural solitude.

The artists were especially drawn to the woodland slopes, waterfalls, and the tapestry of tall trees growing among towering crags and mossy terraces. These scenes held a fascination and appeal to all who admired beauty, form and colour. The crofts (tyddyn) tucked among grey rocky outcrops and trees were also popular subjects.

Betws-y-coed unfolded its charms invitingly, and while the writers entrusted their praise of the place to words it was the devoted artists who captured the attractions of the locality on canvas and transmitted these to a wider public. Nor were the postcard firms going to be left behind in the exploitation process. Once they had become established they promptly portrayed those familiar eminent village attractions — Swallow Falls, Fairy Glen, Miners' Bridge — and added considerable advertisement to the village and its "showpieces" through distribution and communication. A few familiar scenes were even depicted on cigarette cards issued in a series of sets by a leading tobacco company.

The parish contained some of the finest scenery in the country. Both south and north beyond the crags overlooking the village stretched miles of rugged moorland and rock ridges reaching to the foothill territory on the eastern flanks of the high mountains of Snowdonia. There were lakes too and an abundance of changing vistas in all directions. Consequently the village became the base for those eager to explore such

An old print of Betws-y-coed

excellent scenery and take themselves off into the solitude and repose of the hinterland.

The hotels provided leisure and comfort. Furthermore they arranged excursions in their own horse-drawn omnibuses, pony traps and two-horse wagonettes. At one time the Waterloo hotel ran three horse-drawn coaches to Beddgelert and Llanberis and a round trip from Betws-y-coed to Porthmadog, Blaenau Ffestiniog and Dolwyddelan. For these trips relays of horses were kept at places en route and changed where necessary. Generally these horses were bought from Ireland before Easter, trained for a few weeks before the tourist season started and then sold at the end of September or early October.

The Royal Oak hotel also ran horse-drawn coaches to Beddgelert and Llanberis, but the Gwydyr and Glan Aber hotels contented themselves with less ambitious excursions — taking their passengers by two horse-wagonettes to various local places of interest — Fairy Glen, Beaver Pool, Miners' Bridge.

There was considerable rivalry between the drivers and coachmen employed by the hotels with each determining to try and outdo the others by wile and surreptitious acts. Traces and reins were cut, wheel spokes damaged and drivers' seats dismantled. Some drivers even altered the starting times of their rivals' coaches by posting up false notices in the hotel foyers. Behind the scenes it would appear to have been something of a cut-throat occupation, but fortunately it was confined to minor acts of peevishness rather than downright aggression.

In 1899 the Betws-y-coed Urban District Council issued no less than twenty-seven carriage and drivers' licenses to applicants eager to ply their vocation during the increasingly busy tourist season.

The advent of the Conwy Valley railway line from Llandudno Junction to Betws-y-coed meant that the village would be accessible to a considerably larger number of visitors henceforth during the summer season. It became normal for several excursion trains a day to arrive at the station and permit hundreds of visitors to alight to spend a day among the attractions of the village. (See also Wakes Week). The station remained a terminus for eleven years until the line was extended to Blaenau Ffestiniog in 1879 for goods traffic and 1881 for passenger service.

By the beginning of hostilities in 1914 Betws-y-coed had unfolded its many natural assets to an increasingly appreciative public, and the reputation of the village as an established holiday resort was assured.

THE ENDURING YEARS

A near fifty year association with Betws-y-coed affords me pride and gratitude for its contribution to my own life. I was only four and a half years old when I came here in 1925 with my parents. My father had been appointed to take charge of the recently established Gwydir forest and during the next twenty years or so he was closely associated with several village activities — vice-chairman of the football club in the early thirties, a village councillor for many years, and

*Jane Jones, in Welsh costume,
her souvenir stall in Betws*

Chairman of the local British Legion branch.

I attended the village school and my nostalgic memories are all associated with Betws-y-coed when it had long become an established tourist location, requiring no further advertising to proclaim its popularity.

There was a quality of composure in those days of the late 1920's and through the 1930's, inherited, I suspect, from Victorian and Edwardian ages. A high degree of intregrity existed in the village during my schooldays and respect for its local farm and forest characters — characters such as Edwin, Will Herb, Ben Jones 'Rhiwgri' and others.

Recollections of village life over fifty years ago are undimmed in my memories, but alas! that is an age that has passed forever. Still, one can feel sorrow for what the village has forfeited since that period. . .the butcher's shop with the polished meat hooks and sawdust-carpeted floor; the chemist with those oriental-shaped bottles filled with solutions of all colours from bright pink to tangerine standing in a row on the highest shelf; the two grocery shops with their gleaming bacon slicers and aroma of cheeses, condiments and fresh farm butter; the corn mill in Mill street, in Mr Robert's care, and last in use in 1940; the police court; the small, dark corner shop at Pont-y-Pair in the centre of the village, stocked with anything from hob-nailed boots to thick woollen underwear, from a packet of pins to a pair of bootlaces; the Llugwy tearooms (kept by the Misses Atkinson) who served you with home-baked soda or treacle scones, assorted fruit cake, bread and butter, jam and honey, and a large pot of tea all for 1/9d; the station master and his staff and the bustle of the goods yards, and the proud, clean frontage to the station with its cosy restaurant; our cheerful coal merchants and hauliers from Royal Oak farm; the rival taxi owners meeting the trains and glaring at one another as they whisked passengers off to the local beauty attractions; Judges, the small but well stocked library; the local smithy at Green Bank; the Riverside tennis courts. . .To-day I look back and miss the rousing intimacies of our 1930's village life — the wiles of our local (much respected) poachers, be they stalking fish or fowl; the ruses of our errant vagrants and gypsies, who biding their opportunity, wandered into people's gardens, severed a few ash branches, and a day or two later came round selling pegs made from those same branches to the householder at a dozen pegs for sixpence; the chatter and banter of the forest smallholders' wives when they shopped or helped out at church and chapel festivities; the arrival of the excursion trains packed with the cheerful, generous Lancashire folk on their 'Wakes Weeks' outings. . .

Ah! my Betws! I know I'm grateful for all those memories of a youth spent with you when village life comprised a cavalcade of readily identifiable rural characters — loveable, inoffensive and civil — whose exploits recorded that age when life's values held solid foundation, accountable precepts, and a very caring community.

'The tender grace of a day that is dead
Will never come back to me'.

The present day offers an abundant choice of facilities for the visitor. The village's reputation for accommodation, catering and hospitality — gained a century or so ago — remains well in evidence and the local places of interest and repute retain the distinction given to them by Victorian artists and writers. The village backdrop maintains its wood-clad hillsides and protruding crags. Betws-y-coed is busier than ever it was in the past and the season for visitors has extended to almost every month in the year. Enduring years indeed! The village shops disclose all the assorted attractions of vocations alert to the embracing tentacles of modern tourism, where one can purchase an attractive range of souvenirs and garments, outdoor sport and camping equipment, confectionery, paintings and works of art — alas! though — in 1989, no reels of cotton or a pair of bootlaces or a selection of nails and screws.

It is a village of vitality, its bounties presented in good taste. And within the parish boundaries you can explore its ancient past among moss-clad rocks and crags and follow the occasional ancient pathways. Betws-y-coed is a gateway to the inner bastions of Snowdonia, that mountain massif that thwarted so many invaders in the past.

"Live on my Betws for a thousand years more!
Welcome allcomers to your forest-skirted door;
For what you bestow are pleasures quite secure,
And memories of beauty to abidingly endure."

A

ABERLLYN MINE

About half-way up the public footpath from Betws-y-coed to Llyn Parc and just off the route, the remains of this mine can be seen. The footpath itself was used last century by lead miners working at this mine and by others employed in mines higher up on the plateau. In more recent times the wives of the forest smallholders struggled up this path with heavily laden baskets on their way home from the weekly market in Llanrwst.

Aberllyn was primarily a zinc producing mine although lead was extracted as well, much of it over 80% pure. At intervals between 1869-1904 over 2,500 tons of zinc were extracted, and in 1900 over 200 miners were employed here. The mill had been a very substantial structure with seven floors stepped down the hillside, and the outlines of tramways and chutes are still visible to-day. In one adit, lamp brackets fixed at intervals into the rock and the outline of tramway sleepers can be seen.

On the fourth floor the concrete machinery foundations are still in place, and below on the fifth floor are two well preserved concrete buddle pits with their attendant feed channels.

On some of the mine spoil heaps and one or two of the mill floors both Alpine Pennycress and Sea Campion are growing.

The Aberllyn mine closed in liquidation in 1921.

As with every old mine no attempt should be made to enter the adits and great care taken to keep well away from open shafts and stopes.

ABERLLYN RAVINE

A little further up the footpath from the mine a short, spectacular stretch of scenery is reached. Here, the route is enclosed by rugged, precipitous cliffs, with heather ledges and shallow terraces. The ivy-wrapped fissures and clefts high under the eastern crags across the stream were the haunt of raven and buzzard in the early years of forestry here, and polecats were quite common.

The huge Parc fire of 1938 (see Forest Fires) started along the rugged slopes on the left as one ascends the path, and tree trunks and boulders, loosened by the heat crashed down into the ravine, providing an added hazard to the weary firefighters.

As one emerges from the ravine the fields of Aberllyn cottage come into view, and across the stream the ruins of the mine smithy are observed. The walls are unsafe — for safety's sake view this from a distance.

ANGLING

Apart from the pleasures and challenges posed by rod and line, the angler based in Betws-y-coed is given the opportunity for relaxation and observation within valley, woodland and moorland settings of rich variety and considerable beauty.

Salmon have bred in the Conwy, Lledr and Llugwy rivers for centuries, but spring running fish were not introduced until 1920, when Mr Connell Smith of Gwydyr Hotel obtained eggs from Thurso in Scotland and introduced them to a hatchery he built on the Afon Lledr. A decade later these fish and their progeny were returning to the river in April and May.

The locality's claim to angling fame is in having not only good runs of salmon but also excellent runs of sea trout (sewin); this implies that if river levels are too low or the weather too bright for successful salmon or sewin fishing during the day, there are, at least, reasonable prospects for sewin fishing at night.

In the olden days netting was undertaken on the rivers, and coracles were used on the Conwy and on pools in the Lledr and Llugwy rivers, and on a few of the local lakes. There was a salmon trap below Ty'n-y-berth and another a little way above the Black Pool. Both were removed between 1856 and 1866.

An unconfirmed, near-record catch with rod and line of an Atlantic salmon was made in 1892. The fish weighed 46lbs and was caught on the Conwy river a ½ mile or so north of

*Lloyd M. Parry, Tan Lan, Betws-y-coed, with a 36½ lb salmon
he caught in the Conwy river in Betws-y-coed in 1941.
(Photo: Gwydyr Fisheries)*

Betws-y-coed. Reputed to be the largest sea-trout caught
weighed nearly 22 lbs. This was in 1946.

Gwydyr Hotel, in the centre of the village, controls much of
the local river fishing and is responsible for the issue of full
season, weekly or daily tickets.

In 1988 the total number of salmon caught was 325, the
largest one weighing 22lbs. Sea-trout total was 150, 16lbs
being the largest fish caught. In 1987, 267 salmon were caught
and 232 sea-trout successfully landed.

Fishing charges for the seasing 1989 included:-
Full season tickets for salmon — £1,000

Full season tickets for salmon and sea-trout — £1,200
Weekly tickets for salmon and sea-trout from
March-May — £100
Weekly tickets for salmon and sea-trout from
August-October — £180
Sea-trout tickets — Weekly — £80
Hire of fishing tackle (Rods and Reel) — £6 per day.

The Betws-y-coed Fishing Club is locally run and includes angling on some lakes and along sections of the Llugwy river. Tickets and all relevant information may be obtained from Tan-Lan Restaurant, Betws-y-coed.

The arboretum, Betws-y-coed

ARBORETUM

This is located alongside the A5 some 300 yards west of Swallow Falls hotel, and is linked with the picnic place called Cae'n-y-Coed (Field in the Wood). Here, there is ample accommodation for car parking and a toilet block is available. Paths lead the visitor among a collection of labelled exotic conifers, and a pamphlet is obtainable describing these. When the upper part of the arboretum is reached, good views of the Llugwy valley are revealed.

Many species were planted in the early 1950's among natural scrub growing on the area, and most of the latter had to be carefully thinned or felled to permit space for the introduced species to develop and reveal their natural form and outline.

ARTIST'S WOOD

A footbridge along Forest Walk 4 leads the visitor into this attractive corner of Gwydir forest.

Comprised mainly of uneven-aged Beech, some of considerable age and stature, the remainder younger and the product of natural regeneration, this distinctive piece of woodland was a favourite haunt of several respected artists of last century, among them Cox, Creswick, Pickering and Gastineau.

The area contains a range of mosses covering rocks and tree trunks, and near the centre of the grove a standing stone

Artist's Wood bridge

commemorates the planting of the first 100,000 acres of forest by the Forestry Commission in North Wales.

At one time this wood was a favourite haunt of the red squirrel, and the rare and elusive woodcock has bred in the past on the fringes of the area.

The spectacular autumn colouring ranges from bronze to russet and provides a vivid contrast to the adjacent deep green canopy of Douglas fir.

AVERAGE ANNUAL RAINFALL

For the village the annual average rainfall lies between 45-50 inches. In late Spring and early Summer, during the months of April, May and June, the parish often experiences its lightest rainfall, and in spite of the prevalence of April showers that month can be minimally drier than May.

At Betws-y-coed, May June and July are frequently far drier than the popular holiday month of August.

On Snowdon, one of the wettest areas in the United Kingdom, the rainfall is over 200 inches in a year.

B

BEAVER BRIDGE (PONT-YR-AFANC)

This bridge, located in a very picturesque setting near Fairy Glen, is reputed to have been built about 1803 by the sons of an innkeeper whose premises stood where Betws-y-coed railway station is situated to-day. It carried the old route across Afon Conwy before Waterloo bridge was built in 1815. Beaver bridge is a single, nearly semi-circular stone arch with a seventy foot span.

In June 1803 a four-wheeled carriage owned by a Mr Wynne appears to have been the first vehicle across the bridge. To-day, in far less leisurely style, traffic follows the A470 across the bridge en route for Dolwyddelan, Blaenau Ffestiniog and mid and south Wales.

Beaver Pool and Bridge

BEAVER POOL (LLYN-YR-AFANC)

By following the by-road behind Waterloo hotel, the visitor can look down on this impressive and attractive pool immediately downstream from Beaver bridge. On a summer's day, with sunshine sparkling on its water, Beaver pool presents a scene of much charm; on the other hand what a sombre, sinister appearance it displays when a wild winter storm envelops it in gloom.

It is deepest at its upper end and, in season, salmon may be observed in its shallower waters, either in repose or swimming idly upstream.

Beaver pool is a little below a hundred feet above sea level, and slightly downriver from it there used to be an ancient ford called Rhyd-y-Gwyniedyn (Ford of Sewin).

The origin of the name Beaver pool? A long time ago beavers probably did inhabit this pool and made use of the alders growing on some of the riverbanks, but the ancient story-tellers hereabouts would have us know that the pool at one time was the home of a beaver of monstrous proportions.

Hunted by local people its skin proved too tough to be pierced by spears or arrows, and thwarted time and again, they finally called up a fair village maiden to sing to it from the bank. The beaver emerged from the water and listened, enchanted, until it fell asleep at the edge of the pool. Up came a group of hunters with ropes and nets and captured it, and with the aid of two oxen the monster was dragged over the mountains to faraway Llyn Glaslyn where it vanished into its dark waters and was not seen again.

BIRD HABITATS

The parish contains four distinct bird habitats — the sheltered valleys, the steep, rocky hillsides, the open park-like character of the small farmsteads and the fragmented moorland terrain. Within these four habitats different forest conditions prevail — meadowland, glades, stream edges, newly planted areas, mixed conifer and broadleaved species, and tall, near mature timber.

Bird activities (nesting, feeding, singing, preening, roosting) are confined to four zones — ground cover, shrub layer, tree trunks and primary branches, and the crowns of trees. By taking the natural habitats found within the parish, including lakes, the range of birdlife may be followed.

One should remember however, that several species, including the raven, buzzard, blackbird, jay, magpie, robin, wren and wood-pigeon may be observed in flight or heard in song in more than one area and are not confined to a single habitat.

HABITAT TYPE

A SELECTION OF BIRDS TO OBSERVE

(a) Felled woodland areas. There is light and space and a strong growth of natural vegetation. Cover from left-over branchwood; such areas are good open hunting grounds for some birds of prey.

Stonechat; whinchat; robin; wren; tree pipit; skylark; kestrel.

(b) Stream and riverbank. Often with overhanging broadleaved tree cover.

Grey wagtail; dipper; tree creeper; water-pipit; wren.

(c) Moorland and lakes. Open heather ridges, patchy conifer growth; a gorse/bilberry vegetation association; marshy hollows; stunted oak, birch, rowan growth on some areas.

Mallard; moorhen; little grebe; buzzard; curlew; raven; kestrel; meadow-pipit; skylark; blackgame.

(d) Mature conifer forest and areas of oak and other mixed deciduous species reaching maturity or well established on hillsides.

Woodpigeon; jay; magpie; chaffinch; tawny owl; nuthatch; blue tit; coal tit; great tit; green-woodpecker; sparrow-hawk; blackbird.

The visitor may well observe other species within these habitats — if so it will be a bonus. Don't be disappointed if you fail to see many of these listed species — just return another day and enjoy hours of exploration and observation in the Betws woods.

BORROW, GEORGE

The author of *Wild Wales* was born in 1803 and grew up with two dominant characteristics — a passion for wandering and a gift of mastering strange tongues. He became one of the most individual writers of the Victorian era, and though never an accurate philological scholar, he possessed marvellous powers of picking up foreign speech.

By the age of 29, Borrow — then living in Norwich — contrived to learn Welsh on Sundays from a Welsh-born groom, studied Danish in the Guildhall library, took lessons in Hebrew from a Jew, in Spanish and Italian from a French émigré, and he read German with William Taylor, a clever but dissolute man of letters in the Cathedral City.

Borrow rambled about the countryside with gypsies and took himself off in a tinker's cart. As a linguist he was introduced to the British and Foreign Bible Society and soon found himself learning Manchu and eventually producing a Manchu New Testament in 1835.

He made friends with all sorts and conditions of men — smugglers, priests, peasants, ambassadors and vagabonds. He had conversations with the Prime Minister of Spain and the Archbishop of Toledo, and he saw the inside of more than one Spanish prison. In 1851 his book 'Lavengro' was published — a most fascinating open-air book, followed six years later by the publication of 'Romany Rye'.

George Borrow travelled extensively through the Principality in the middle of last century and his experiences are chronicled in 'Wild Wales'. He astonished many residents of North Wales by his command of the ancient tongue of the Cymry, which he liked to express himself in to the natives. Some of his passages are perhaps a little long-winded, but his love and admiration for Wales is never in doubt. When in the Conwy valley he came across that "rare and curious book" — 'The History of the Gwydir Family' written by Sir John Wynne of Gwydir early in the 17th century, he likened it to an Icelandic saga.

It was in 1854 when he mentions Betws-y-coed in 'Wild Wales' — "crossed over an ancient bridge and passed through a small town and found myself in a beautiful valley with majestic hills on either side."

An honest out-of-doors, open-air writer, George Borrow, spent many dismal solitary hours in his old age and in the end died quite alone.

BUTTERFLIES

Sheltered valleys with damp meadows and heath-like slopes among patches of natural oak afford almost ideal conditions for many varieties of butterfly, and within the parish it is possible to see as great a profusion as in any south country woodland, despite the variable weather in this area. In the right season butterflies can be seen around village gardens and in open spaces within the surrounding woodland. Of these the Common Blue, Holly Blue, Small Copper, and Orange Tip are frequently observed, and the Green Hairstreak can be found along the rough hillsides clothed with bilberry and dwarf gorse.

The Marsh Fritillary is locally fairly common on suitable marshy ground on the uplands.

C

CADWALAD Y CLOGWYN (CADWALAD OF THE CRAG)

This notorious character lived in a hut at the summit of a crag above the present day railway tunnel opposite to Pont Llyn-yr-Afanc, (Beaver Pool Bridge).

A footpath and forest walk (No 2) pass through terrain once very familiar to this character. The fields of Mynydd Bychan (small mountain) were close by his hut. Cadwalad was a turner by trade, working his lathe — as was the custom in those days — by means of a strong, bent rod. By all accounts throughout his life he had been cruel and vindictive, and retaliated maliciously against all those who in the slightest manner offended him, whether intentionally or innocently.

He was crafty and cunning, and by these means successfully eluded being brought to justice for various misdeeds. Arson and hamstringing cattle were his principal weapons of revenge, and in a single night he once set fire to four properties — Cwm Dreiniog, Ty'n-y-Berth, Llawrynys and Craig Glan Conwy, all within the parish. At the last dwelling the inhabitants only just escaped with their lives, the cowhouse being burned to the ground and the tethered cattle within it perishing in the blaze.

During his last hours as he lay sick in his hut, Cadwalad y Clogwyn mumbled over the vicious misdeeds he had perpetrated in his lifetime, and in an appeal for forgiveness cried out: "Let lose the cows! They are burning! Let them lose! Woe is me! Alas the day wherein I was born! I am sinking fast!"

He was buried at Betws-y-coed on June 20th, 1804.

CATTLE DROVERS AND DEALERS

Up to the early years of the 19th century store cattle (Runts) were sent in droves from the Betws-y-coed district, the Gwydir estate and other parts of the upper Conwy valley, some to available markets, others to the fattening pastures of the Midland counties. The men responsible for all the undertakings to do with cattle trade were the drovers and dealers. They were respected and trusted by the poor country folk; they brought currency into the heart of the remote country districts around Betws-y-coed; they were the Argonauts of trade and the initiators of country banks.

The drovers who accompanied cattle herds were the only people making regular journeys to the English markets; often they were entrusted with responsible commissions, and were the bearers of news of Parliament to the isolated dwellers of the Gwydir district. Furthermore, they brought back samples of seeds of special field crops and tree cuttings, both of which would prove beneficial to the dweller of the 'tyddyn'.

By uniting their herds, drovers were able to travel in company and a degree of safety (rather like the wagon train occupants in the pioneer days of the old American West). Their routes to the border and beyond were infested with bands of robbers who would assuredly assault a single drover, but would think twice about attacking numbers of herdsmen. Even Bishop Morgan, who translated the Bible into Welsh, and who was born only a short distance from Betws-y-coed, travelled in the company of drovers all the way to London, bearing his precious manuscript for publication.

So valuable was the cattle trade to the upper Conwy valley countryside, that in 1642, the outbreak of the Civil War, a petition was sent to Charles 1 by the Wynns of Gwydir, asking for the free passage and safe conduct of cattle through the Royalist lines. This trade, they declared, was the support of hundreds of families in the upland regions who sowed little or no corn, but depended entirely for their livelihood on the rearing and sale of cattle, with perhaps some wool or cloth.

In 1763 beef from the locally raised cattle sold at Smithfield market at 5 pence a pound.

CATTLE FAIRS

Before Betws-y-coed became widely recognised, visitors beyond the Conwy valley were few and far between. The principal attraction to the village by outsiders in those early times was its two cattle fairs, held on May 15th and December 3rd. On these dates, farm stock dealers came to inspect and purchase cattle raised on local tyddyn pastures or brought in from farther afield. The selected beasts were shod and rested before beginning the long journey to the border markets and quite often to the London cattle markets.

CATRIN MATHEW

At a pool called Ty'n-y-Cae (nowadays a popular stretch of water for anglers), where the Conwy and Lledr rivers converge below Pont Lledr, there used to be many years ago a ferryboat kept by an old woman named Catrin Mathew. Evidence of this could apparently be verified by an inscription "CM" on the stone from which passengers used to step to and from the boat. In the stone was a square hole with a piece of an iron peg broken in it — to this peg Catrin and others must have been in the habit of fastening the ferry boat.

By all accounts Catrin could be perverse at times. To summon her a horn had to be blown from the other side of the river and if the weather was unkind, or Catrin was in one of her bad moods, or she realised there was only one passenger and her effort would be too great and her reimbursement too small, she would ignore the call and retreat into her dwelling, leaving the traveller stranded.

One dark night, so the story is related, Ellis Williams, a native of a neighbouring parish, blew loudly on the horn as an intimation that he wished to cross. Realising he was alone, Catrin ignored his summons and left him to his own devices. To her surprise however, a minute or so later Ellis Williams appeared at her door having swam across the river. Vexed, wet and thoroughly annoyed he claimed derisively to have crossed on a bramble and told her that henceforth the devil take her, her ferryboat and the summoning horn.

Catrin Mathew wasn't altogether cowed by his ill-humour

(after all she'd suffered much abuse over her non co-operation on many occasions in the past), but she was quite startled when a neighbour told her later that Ellis Williams had jumped off Pont-y-Pair bridge when the river was in flood, and allowed the current to take him down to Llanrwst where he attended the cattle market.

Local tradition claimed that Ellis Williams "owing to some peculiarity in his bodily constitution" could not sink.

What further proof of this "peculiar bodily constitution" would anyone require after this near four-mile ride on water when the river was in full spate? Little wonder Catrin Mathew was kept speculating about a crossing on a bramble one dark night. . .

Clogwyn Cyrau

CLOGWYN CYRAU (CORNER PRECIPICE)

To the north this crag dominates the village and is a prominent feature 600 ft above sea level. A public footpath (The Jubilee Path) follows an older track up the steep hillslope to the summit, from which splendid views across valley and village are experienced and many landscape features readily identified.

CONWY RIVER & CONWY VALLEY (AFON CONWY A DYFFRYN CONWY)

Born almost 1500 feet above sea level in Llyn Conwy and enriched by various small tributaries emerging from the bogland in the northern half of the Migneint moors, this river gathers pace in a narrow upland vale by Ysbyty Ifan, bears sharply to the west near Pentrefoelas, rushes over Conwy Falls and through the rocky gorge of Fairy Glen, beneath Waterloo bridge, and then meanders regally down the Conwy valley to the sea. It becomes tidal in its lower reaches, and near Betws-y-coed three tributaries swell its waters — Afon Machno, Afon Lledr and Afon Llugwy. A part of the Conwy's mid-region course is characterised by reed beds along its banks.

Llyn Conwy, with a surface area of 97 acres and in an area where the annual rainfall exceeds 82 inches, has been renowned for its lusty trout and the former Lords of Penrhyn were pretty strict about preserving them. To-day the National Trust administer the property and are just as zealous in conserving all natural features. Just below its source, and while still in its infancy, the Conwy's banks have been enriched with the lovely globe flower in Springtime, and early in the same season flocks of curlew have been known to attend the area to found new families.

At one time the country around Llyn Conwy belonged to the Knights of St John of Jerusalem; they had a preceptory at Ysbyty Ifan (The Hospital of John). Until the Dissolution of the Monastries, the whole lordship of Ysbyty Ifan was a sanctuary where the King's writ did not run, and the rule of the Knights was not strong enough to prevent the district becoming a den of outlaws who ravished the countryside for twenty miles around, and were only finally defeated and scattered by a group of local soldiery led by members of the Wynne family of Gwydir.

Conwy valley extends from south to north for nearly 20 miles. The main valley has a flat alluvial floor of between a half and three-quarters of a mile in width, which reaches only 30 feet above sea level even at Betws-y-coed, 14 miles inland.

It is not primarily a glaciated U-shaped valley or an

The Conwy Valley

over-deepened valley, but a fault-shattered belt which pre-glacial rivers were able to excavate rapidly after changes in base-level. To the west the flanks of the Conwy valley rise very steeply; the slopes are considerably less steep to the east, and the landscape is much softer and less rugged.

Afon Conwy is one of the finest salmon and trout rivers in Wales and is favoured by anglers from near and far who come to test their skills in its charitable waters.

CONWY VALLEY RAILWAY MUSEUM

This specially designed building has been erected in the old goods yard of the village station. Here, in the heyday of the steam trains there was considerable bustle and activity — goods trains bringing in items such as farm equipment, fertiliser, animal foodstuff, coal, mining equipment, and building material, and outgoing trains conveying slate, timber, farm stock, minerals and nursery transplants to distant destinations. The goods yard closed in 1964.

Within the museum there are exhibits portraying many aspects of railway life and work, with special emphasis on the railways of N. Wales. One exhibit has been constructed by a local resident who is a railway enthusiast.

Rides are available on a miniature railway which circles the area around the museum. Light refreshments may be obtained in a coach drawn up alongside a section of the original goods yard platform.

CORACLES

Up until about 1884 these were used for fishing on the Conwy, Lledr and Llugwy rivers and on several lakes in the locality.

Ioan Glan Lledr in a coracle on the Conwy River
at the end of the 19th century

COX, DAVID

The premier artist associated with Betws-y-coed and the immediate locality. The son of a blacksmith, Cox was born in a Birmingham suburb in 1783. He started painting scenery in a London theatre at four shillings a square yard, and after tuition by John Varley, an eminent water colourist, he discovered Betws-y-coed on his first visit to Wales. Thereafter the village became his Mecca. He stayed at the Royal Oak hotel and painted the famous signboard, which is now hung in the hotel foyer, indicating the name of the hostelry. Cox worked exclusively in water colours until he was past fifty, but after 1839 he devoted himself to painting in oils.

CRAIG-Y-DDERWEN (OAK ROCK)

A Country House Hotel overlooking Afon Conwy. Formerly a private property built about 1882 by a Dr Thomas who sold the house to a Mr Challinor, a solicitor from Hanley, who enlarged it. Thereafter it became a private hotel, and during the Second World War it was requisitioned by the War Department and used as HQ of the Cambrian Sub-District.

Craig-y-Dderwen

D

DAVIES, WALTER

This distinguished chronicler reported that between 1754 and

1760 some £50,000 worth of oak timber was felled and floated down the river Conwy from the parishes of Penmachno and Betws-y-coed. For those times this was a great amount of money, and much of the produce from the woods was loaded aboard ship at Conwy and taken to naval yards for conversion. By 1805 — some forty-five years later — a 74-gun ship of the line in Nelson's day required over two and a half thousand tons of timber sawn and carved from perhaps 700 large oak trees.

DINAS

Three topographical features bear this title in the vicinity of Betws-y-coed. The old Welsh word, *dinas* means a 'Celtic hill-fort' in English.

Pen-y-Dinas: This is a prominent crag immediately behind the Swallow Falls hotel. The summit is just over 800 ft above sea level, and translated this would be 'Top of the Fort'.

Clogwyn Dinas: A prominent crag immediately above and north of Miners' Bridge in the Llugwy valley. Height above 700 ft above sea level. Translated this would mean 'Fort Cliff'.

Craig Dinas: The A5 climbs a steep hill to the south east of Betws-y-coed. The bare rock of Craig Dinas towers above the road — translated this would mean 'Fort Rock'.

DIOSGYDD NURSERY

Situated on the north side of Afon Llugwy and almost opposite to the Swallow Falls, this productive forest nursery was established in 1925. In it, over 16,000,000 coniferous and broadleaved tree species were raised between 1925 - 46 for planting in Gwydir forest and other forests in Wales and England. The nursery was abandoned in 1948 and its five or so acres planted with a tree crop, but evidence of the old paths and some of the plots are still visible to-day.

DISTINGUISHED VISITORS

Among those who at one time or another have stayed in the village — some overnight only, others for a longer visit — include the poets Shelley and Wordsworth, Mathew Arnold,

Hoeing in Diosgydd Nursery.
Will Herb's Lantern tree is on the right of the photograph.

Charles Darwin, Charles Kingsley, The Queen of Siam, Alexander Bell (inventor of the telephone), Sir Edward Elgar, Monsieur A. Sartiax (one time President of the French Railways), George Borrow, Thomas Pennant, one member of the Rockfeller family, and Wilhelmina Stitch who wrote "The Fragrant Minute" here at Betws-y-coed.

On June 1st, 1956, Prince Philip, Earl of Merioneth (Welsh title of the Duke of Edinburgh) was brought by Royal Train to the village station on his way to the Snowdonia National Recreation Centre at Capel Curig. He spent some time outside the station meeting veterans of the local British Legion branch.

'THE FRAGRANT MINUTE'
(Written at Betws-y-coed)

'Oh! Foolish tourists to rush here just for an hour or two,
I'd like to stay a twelve-monthed year, with not a thing to do
But walk this beauty spot of Wales, this Chapel-in-the-wood,
Until I knew these mingling vales as beauty lovers should.
Until I knew these tree-clad hills as friend can know a friend,
These rivers, streams and falls and rills — this beauty without end.

To have a year in which to learn the language of the Swallow Falls!
It makes the leaping spirit yearn to answer its wild calls;
And time to sit beneath a bough in this cool Fairy Glen,
And wait and wait, as I do now, to see the fairy men.
Oh! Foolish tourists who rush here for just an hour or two,
I've had a day, I'd like a year, Betws-y-Coed with you!'
                                        Wilhelmina Stitch.

DULWICH COLLEGE PREP SCHOOL

A large number of these young pupils were evacuated from
London to the village in 1940 and remained here until 1945.
They were based at the Royal Oak hotel and had some
classrooms in the Royal Oak stables (now the village
Information Centre). The pupils undertook considerable
forestry work as the School's contribution to the war effort.
This work was done on two afternoons a week and each boy
was paid sixpence a time for his afternoons' contribution.
Wisely, it was considered too great a risk to provide axes or
reaping hooks for use by the boys! So each pupil had his
curved pruning saw with which to prune the lower conifer
branches within the plantations. Over 200 acres were
completed by 1945.

Members of school staff and many of the senior boys helped
fight the 1942 forest fire near Llyn Parc, and a plaque was
erected to commemorate their forest activities, at the side of
the by-road just beyond Coedcynhelier. This may be seen
to-day, and behind, is a plot of conifers planted by the pupils
before they left Betws-y-coed.

A plaque in St Mary's Church commemorates those
members of staff and pupils who attended there to worship
during the war years, and a book "School Errant" by the
headmaster, Mr J. H. Leakey, describes many events of
school life during the years spent in the village.

E

EDWIN

If you follow Forest Walk 5 along the northern bank of Afon

Llugwy, deep in the heart of Gwydir forest, you will come across a small group of Silver Fir with a painted post at the base of one tree. This tree was planted in the early 1930's by a man called Edwin. In a sense it is his memorial, for though Edwin did nothing in his life to warrant a static marble sculpture being erected in his memory, his "statue" increases yearly in height, girth and volume and is not a cold, inanimate object but a vigorous, resin-scented organism. And where the former collect grime and debris on their statues in the centre of busy thoroughfares, Edwin's is in a quiet unsullied location near the banks of Afon Llugwy with a forest floor of moss, fern and bracken to support it.

He was a small, thin man with a pronounced stoop and everyone in the village called him Edwin. Quiet, courteous and slow of speech, he had acquired his hunched bearing by digging people's gardens, weeding countless lawns and tending herbaceous borders for the village hoteliers for over forty years. A very talented gardener, Edwin had a passion for soil and all growing plants; his scarred and calloused fingers reverently handling blooms and root systems alike with utmost tenderness.

But the village economy in the late 1920's mirrored world-wide recession of the times. No longer could people afford a full time gardener and reluctantly Edwin's former employers were forced to part with him — "He was a good gardener as good gardeners go, and as good gardeners go, he went".

Edwin was jobless. For weeks gloom, impatience and hurt pride dwelt within the walls of his neat little cottage and the discarded talents of the little man appeared to be no longer required. Then, one morning, a friend called at the cottage and informed him that the Head Forester was looking for two or three men to work in the forestry nursery at Diosgydd, near Swallow Falls, "Go for the job Edwin bach. Tending young trees'll be like tending shrubs. Go an' see the Head Forester to-day man".

Edwin did. The Head Forester was aware of Edwin's talents and accepted him without question. He began work the following Monday morning and the nursery foreman was warned about one thing — Edwin communicated verbally with his plants and spoke to them alound on many occasions. This had no bearing on the quality of his work the foreman was assured, nor did it signify the early stages of senile decay. It was innocent habit that was all, and the foreman was to ignore it.

Edwin quickly earned the respect of his colleagues, his foreman and the Head Forester for his obvious ability. Yet nobody in that nursery could ever quite reconcile these virtues with the little man's conversations with his trees. He would stoop over a group of pine or spruce whilst hoeing between the transplant lines in the summer and exhort this or that tree to, "speed up your growth" or "raise your head higher towards the sky, my little one" or, "you're looking a bit off colour to-day, there'll be a shower along pretty soon n'ay".

His colleagues would look up and nudge one another and grin — not with malice but in respectful response to conduct that they would never quite become used to. When in the early-thirties Edwin planted his retirement tree close by Afon Llugwy it was an eighteen-inch transplant raised in Diosgydd nursery. Doubtless he had spoken to it at some time, perhaps chiding it if he considered growth was slow.

To-day it towers over a hundred feet tall, a graceful monarch of the forest giving shade to the resting walker and shelter to roosting birds. Edwin would be proud of his tree one feels sure, for it has, over half a century, "kept rising its head towards the sky". It is a living, growing memorial to a simple, dedicated, kindly man — and it gathers no grime.

Perhaps Edwin is still whispering his exhortations to it from some distant, fragrant garden.

EFFIGY

A recumbent effigy of an armoured knight may be seen in the chancel of St Michael's church. The knight was Gruffudd ap Dafydd Goch (Griffith, Son of David the Red) and grandson of Prince David. The latter became leader of the Welsh soldiery in the struggle against the forces of Edward 1, but was captured and beheaded at Shrewsbury in 1283.

His grandson, Gruffudd ap Dafydd Goch, campaigned for England as a Knight of the Black prince and was buried with full military honours — the effigy shows him with sword and spurs. His home was at Fedw Deg, a mile or so up the hillside from Lledr bridge, and the path leading up to the house is still known as Llwybr Gruffudd ap Dafydd Goch — Griffith, son of David the Red's path.

ELECTION EXPENSES (1898)

The election expenses for conducting the first Council election came to £7.15.2 (£7.75p).

ELECTRICITY SUPPLY

The authorised undertaking of an electricity supply to Betws-y-coed Urban District Council was sanctioned in 1906 and in 1913 electrically-lit street lighting was introduced.

ELSI LAKE (LLYN ELSI)

This lake, on the moorland plateau south of Betws-y-coed is one of the village's favourite features and has long been popular with visitors and residents alike. It can be reached by a number of public routes which are clearly shown in official guide books and on maps displayed on information boards in the village.

Llyn Elsi is over 700 feet above sea level and from various knolls surrounding it excellent views may be experienced. Planted areas on some sites have, however, restricted panoramas, particularly to the west.

It is a lake of great charm, rocky-walled, with isles and inlets. Tree clad bluffs around the lake contribute colour and variety to the scene. Floating plants may be found and there are a number of sundew-rich bogs along the water's edge.

In 1946 a colony of black-headed gulls became established causing concern to the council fathers of the Principality's smallest Urban District Council by polluting the village's water supply.

A biologist has claimed that in the silt at the bottom of the lake lie many oak and pitchpine stumps, ancient remnants of a past age when the climate was warmer.

Llyn Elsi

Llyn Elsi has always been a favourite expanse of water for anglers and permits are obtainable on daily or weekly terms.

EXPLOSIVES STORE

In 1899, the Betws-y-coed council were asked by the County Council to take over the licensing of Explosives stores in their district. They agreed to do this, and under the 1875 Explosives Act, application for the storage of explosive licenses and registration of premises were made from Aberllyn lead and Zinc mine, Coedmawr Pool lead mine, Hafodlas slate quarry and the village chemist.

The Council granted licenses to all four applicants.

F

FAIRY GLEN

One of the principal natural attractions of the village, and

Fairy Glen

where Wilhelmina Stitch, "waits and waits, to see the fairy men".

Located only a short distance from Beaver bridge, a combination of rapids and cascades on the Conwy river are chanelled into a narrow ravine presenting an impressive and dramatic scene. Wooded banks and rock walls clothed with vegetation add to the charm.

Fairy Glen is reached by a path from Fairy Glen house beside the A470.

FARM CENSUS WITHIN FOREST LAND — 1938

During the Forestry Commission's formative years a number of upland farmsteads and tyddyns (smallholdings) within Betws-y-coed parish were occupied by forest workers who, apart from their occupation in the expanding woodlands, were responsible for tending their stock and overseeing the condition of their land. Indeed, forest and farm combined in close harmony for nearly three decades — and with the demise of the local lead mines and slate quarries, — forestry became the premier source of rural employment within the parish. The added attraction of rearing stock on pastures within the forest was a further reward for the eager tenant despite the hard work involved.

The following seven examples are representative of land use at the time the survey was accomplished (1938). It shows how population on the uplands has decreased considerably over the past fifty years and just how much stock (particularly sheep) could be raised on the average tyddyn or farm where the quality of pasture could only be defined as unfavourable.

Most of the properties are close by forest walks or rambles outlined in brochures or the Betws-y-coed official guide. Over the years, as the dwellings became vacant, the grazing lands were lost to forest, though Diosgydd Uchaf, Hafodlas and Coedmawr still have a good acreage of open pasture.

The remnants of farm outbuildings and the outlines of stone wall boundaries may still be seen within plantations now in occupation of former upland meadowland.

Name of Property	Acreage	No. in family	Cattle	Stock sheep	pigs	horses
Cwm Dreiniog	112	7	11	200	1	-
Mynydd Bychan	58	5	7	50	-	-
Rhiwgri	76	1	-	64	-	-
Hafodlas	94	5	7	60	-	-
Maesnewyddion	98	3	1	90	-	-
Diosgydd Uchaf	54	4	5	90	-	-
Coedmawr	41	4	10	50	-	1

Average per Household — 4
Average per Acreage — 76
Average Cattle number — 6
Average Number of sheep — 86

FIR TREE ISLAND

This feature, just upriver from Pont-y-Pair bridge, is recognised as being one of the village's most photographed and popular scenes. Isolated at times of flood, it is easily reached when the river is low. Famed for its mixed tree colony — comprised of four Western Hemlock, one Japanese Larch, two Spruce, one mature Birch and some scrub oak, alder and birch — the island is effectively displayed at night when illuminations are switched on.

FOREST FIRES

Whatever the cause, an outbreak of fire within a forest exhausts (and often frightens) the personnel combatting it, produces a severe financial loss to the owner and leaves a grievous scar on the landscape for a long while. Furthermore there is a loss of food, cover and habitat for a diverse bird and animal population.

Much of the mid-section of Gwydir forest is within Betws-y-coed parish and during the formative years of forestry it was the steam engine hauling the trains up the steep inclines in the Lledr valley that caused lineside fires to spread to adjacent plantations.

Over the years scores of fires have been fought and extinguished. There is a high risk during hot weather in the holiday season; and at Gwydir the period between late

Fir Tree Island

February and early April can be the most potentially dangerous of all because of (a) drying easterly winds and early Spring drought; (b) the presence of so much dead and inflammable vegetation within the plantations before the beginning of the new growing season; (c) farmers burning adjacent hill land to improve the grazing value for summer when stock are taken up to high pasture.

Major Fires:

The largest outbreak was in the Llyn Parc area on May 11/12, 1938, when flames were swept across the lake by strong winds and destroyed 411 acres of thriving plantations. In those years there were no forest roads to facilitate access and bring up equipment, and there was no National Fire Service. To get to the scene the firefighters had to struggle up steep hillsides and follow narrow paths and cart tracks; exhaustion soon followed as they fought the blaze over some of the roughest terrain in the forest. This fire was subsequently dramatised by BBC Bangor and broadcasted on 30th May, 1938.

A wartime fire occured in 1942 to the west of Llyn Parc and burned 108 acres. Because enemy night bombers used the N. Wales coastline as their route to bomb Merseyside, and pilots could have seen the blazing forest some ten miles inland and be deceived into considering it to be a target area, the firefighters sought resolutely to get the fire under control before nightfall. They failed because the fire burned deep into pockets of peat, but fortunately no German planes appeared. The fire lasted almost a week during a hot interval of weather, flaring up continuously in the deep peat areas, but there were no scares and not a sign of enemy aircraft.

In 1951, 123 acres were lost to the west of Pencraig on the Glyn area. It was after this fire that a programme of forest roads was planned and started, both to provide quick access for emergencies and to facilitate the hauling out of timber.

In 1976, 180 acres were burned, but tree losses were relatively low because much of the terrain was unplanted and a lot of the planted area was in check. The blaze had a dramatic effect but was not a financial disaster.

Four years later a mountain fire between Crafnant and Geirionnydd lakes caused a loss of 180 acres, but here again, much of the area supported only patches of growing timber.

G

GALLERY

Alongside the A5 and only some 50 yards up from Pont-y-pair, this imposing building stands on the site of the first endowed, purpose-built school in the village. (See Sophia Jex-Blake). The gallery displays an attractive and numerous assortment of items for sale, and these include a selection of paintings — some of them of local interest.

GARAGE

In the past, known locally as Green's Garage, the first village garage opened here in 1906. The premises are situated on the by-road leading past 'Spar' stores, to the rear of Waterloo hotel and on to Beaver pool and bridge.

GARTH FALLS WALK

Recipient of a Prince of Wales award in 1976, this walk was prepared for handicapped people of all ages and is suitable for invalid chair occupants, either self-propelled or pushed, the deaf, the blind and the elderly.

A paved surface walk some 300 metres in length, the route follows close to a stream and in part passes beneath tall timber. At the end of the walk an attractive waterfall may be observed from an enclosed area containing several picnic tables. Along the route are seats and passing places, and at intervals on the handrails there are braille embossed plates giving brief information for the blind on what they can feel and touch — such as the trunk of a spruce tree or a clump of heather.

On Thursday, July 22nd, 1976, a simple and moving ceremony marked the official opening of the walk. Mr Arthur Rowlands, an ex-policeman from the Gwynedd Constabulary, who was blinded while making an arrest a few years earlier, cut the ceremonial tape.

Representatives from the Press, BBC, the local Community

Garth Falls Walk

Council and the principal social and disabled organisations were present, and recordings were made for the following day's "Bore da" (Good morning) programme.

Just off the A5 opposite to the entrance to Miner's Bridge, the walk is reached by following the by-road leading slightly uphill for about 100 yards. Parking space is available.

GARTHERYR (EAGLE HILL)

Once a tyddyn (smallholding) with its own limited pasture wrested from the rocky hillsides and its neat stone walls enclosing meadows and a small orchard, all that remains to-day of Gartheryr are its ruins alongside a public footpath leading up to Llyn Elsi from the rear of St Mary's church.

In 1926 it was occupied for a time by a Forestry Commission tenant, but soon became vacant and the adjacent land quickly reverted to heather, gorse and scrub until many years later, a tree crop was planted. Between Gartheryr and St Mary's Church are the remnants of old Gwydir estate woodlands comprised of a mixture of deciduous tree species.

But it was away back in the middle of the 18th century that Gartheryr became more than just a small, obscure tyddyn within the parish. Here, in 1749, under the influence and drive of a certain Ann Jones, who was employed at Cwm Dreiniog, a farm beyond Llyn Elsi, a small congregation of Calvanistic Methodists used to meet once a week. Encouraged by Ann Jones's enthusiasm and dedication, the members' numbers soon increased and a new devotional practice was introduced to the parish and surrounding district.

GEOLOGY & SOILS

When the visitor sets out to explore the countryside around Betws-y-coed one feature of interest will be the nature of the rocks, vegetation and soil which he or she will observe en-route.

The rock formations are the products of activity during the Ordovician Period, 500-400 million years ago. During the mid-Ordovician period much of the United Kingdom was covered by seas and erupting volcanoes. The latter activity occurred over millions of years in N. Wales, where Snowdonia was a low lying island, a magma-filled blister. Great clouds of hot gasses and lava fragments issued from fissures to be quenched by the sea in clouds of steam. A pall of fine ash filled the sky, accompanied by violent thunderstorms. To-day Snowdon is a pile of eroded Ordovician lavas and ashes about one mile thick.

The Ordovician rocks (named after the Ordovices, an ancient Welsh tribe) found within the parish consist of dark-coloured shales, grits and sandstones with many igneous rocks interbedded between them. A thick wedge of Rhyolite (an igneous rock of acid composition) crops out on the slopes of Coed Aberllyn, and Grinllwm slates form a prominent scarp just north of Betws-y-coed and to the east of Llyn Parc.

Fossils formed in these Ordovician rocks include the earliest forms of fish — types very different from those of to-day. Within the district around Betws-y-coed faunas associated with the Ordovician sediments are rarely well preserved and have mostly been deformed.

However a few localities have yielded good fossils of an uncertain age — for example: Cremnorthis Parva (Bryozoa) on a crag east of Pen-yr-Allt Ganol, and stick-like Bryozoa (Bicuspina Spirferoides) on a forestry track north of Llyn Elsi. Both locations are close to forest walks.

By-gone landscapes "come alive" in our minds when we can imagine them as peopled with living things. Most fossils — from a Latin word meaning "things dug up" — consist only of hard substances like tree trunks, tree roots, animal shells, bones or teeth.

Within the parish there is a wide contrast in soils. Alluvium — commonly exposed in the eroded banks of Afon Conwy, up Afon Llugwy as far as Pentre Du and partly up Afon Lledr — consists of clayey sand overlying coarse gravels. This is a valley bottom soil; higher up the hillsides are the upland brown earths which are freely drained soils. On the uplands there are very few locations with peaty gley soils, and only scattered molinia (purple moor grass) bogs.

Ironpan soils (a peaty surface depth overlying a pale-grey layer, below which is a thin band of brown deposited iron) severely restrict tree rooting, but fortunately only appear in a relatively few places.

When the mineral profile is less than 35cm deep over rock the soil type is considered to be skeletal in nature; rooting depth is much restricted and tree growth may be limited or terminated by drought or lack of nutrients.

Three fairly common vegetation types seen on one's travels within the parish are heather, gorse and bracken. An allusion to the quality of soil under these species of vegetation was given by an old hill-farmer and shepherd, who knew every yard of the uplands to the north of Betws-y-coed and had spent nearly a lifetime observing nature's influences in the area. He would say:-

O dan y Rhedyn - Aur	Under Bracken - Gold
O dan yr Eithin - Copr	Under Gorse - Copper
O dan y Grug - Plwm	Under Heather - Lead

The minerals indicated the descending soil values as they applied to the likely grazing worth of land for rearing and feeding stock on the uplands.

GETHIN'S BRIDGE

This huge, imposing viaduct in the Lledr valley carries the railway line from Betws-y-coed to Dolwyddelan and Blaenau Ffestiniog across the A470 about 1¼ miles from Beaver bridge. This impressive undertaking was the work of poet, author and historian Owen Gethin Jones, born in 1816 in the parish of Penmachno. He was a master craftsman, a stone-mason of wide repute and a talented writer. He designed the viaduct himself and constructed it using a minimum number of workmen, undertaking much of the detailed work on his own. Gethin Jones also built the railway station at Betws-y-coed, one of the finest stations in Wales in its day. He died in 1883.

GIANT'S HEAD
(CLOGWYN Y GIGFRAN)

This feature in the Lledr valley can be reached by two routes — by Forest Walk 2, described in a Forestry Commission pamphlet, and by Walk 7 outlined in the official guide to Betws-y-coed.

Viewed from a distance across the valley this sheer cliff bears resemblance, in part, to the outline and features of a human profile. The crag overlooks the railway line from Betws-y-coed to Dolwyddelan, the A470 road between these two places and the river Lledr.

Giant's Head is nearly 500 feet above sea level and every care should be taken at the summit not to approach too close to the edge of the cliff.

GOLF CLUB

This nine-hole golf course is framed in a pleasant 35 acre site to the east of the railway station and is flanked by the rivers Conwy and Llugwy, with wooded hillslopes forming a spectacular backcloth on three sides.

The present course has been laid out on an earlier one which ceased to be played over in 1919 and had only lasted for a few years. During work on the preparation of the present course a golf ball of the old Gutta-Percha type was found in

Gethin's bridge

1975, probably about 60 years old.

Course construction took twelve months to complete and is 2404 yards in length. Par is 32.

The club was opened in 1977 and bears the motto: 'Twyllo arall, twyllo dy hunan' (To deceive others is to deceive thyself).

There is a well appointed clubhouse and refreshment room, and access is over the railway bridge nearly opposite to Midland bank, and thence by St Michael's Church.

GWYDIR FOREST

The forest takes its title from the ancient estate once in possession of the Wynns of Gwydir Castle, and much of the mid-section of the forest is within Betws-y-coed parish. In 1937 Gwydir became a National Forest Park.

The time of crisis arrived for Betws-y-coed's widely acclaimed woodlands during the 1914-18 conflict. The country was acutely short of timber even before this, and with the advent of submarine warfare and the priority given to more vital imports, timber was severely restricted. But it had to be found — and the ring of axe and crunch of toppling trees were soon commonplace sounds along the hillsides surrounding the village much to the residents' chagrin and disquiet. All the best timber was felled and hauled out by teams of horses to sawmills on the outskirts of the village, where they were sawn into required sizes and sent off by rail to their destinations.

The craggy hillsides were left strewn with lopped branches and isolated groups of natural scrub too uneconomic to fell and extract. It was a sorry sight and experience for the village residents, for the landscape had undergone a dramatic change in a matter of a few years.

Under the Forestry Act of 1919 the Forestry Commission became the properly constituted authority to deal with all aspects of forestry within the United Kingdom. While the old woodlands around Betws-y-coed had been mainly deciduous in character and had not been managed or maintained as a commercial enterprise, the new plantations would be mostly of conifers with the objective of management on a commercial

An aerial photograph showing the forested area
around Betws-y-coed

basis, regularly thinned and administered until clear felling became necessary at the end of a rotation (some 60-70 years).

Re-planting of the woodlands round the village began in 1921 and remnants of some of the old woods were incorporated into the newly established plantations, preserving an attractive mixed species appearance across much of the higher valley slopes and creating a diverse forest canopy within the rugged landscape. The critics may well enquire why grow so many conifers? Is there no place for more concentration on the planting of oak, beech and ash? Were not the old woodlands mainly of oak?

Modern commercial needs go a long way to answering these questions. As a nation we use less than one tenth of deciduous species for our industrial requirements; to-day's industry needs readily available, quick-grown supplies of timber.

Coniferous species provide this. Within 20, 30, 40 years (depending on the rotation decided) they can be harvested and the resource made available immediately. On average 2-5 rotations of conifers can be grown to 1 of oak.

Huge mature oak have grown on the Betws-y-coed hillsides — some are still here to-day, massive remnants of a once dense woodland. How old are these still vigorous trees? Confidently one can say 200 years, perhaps more — and just consider how many mature, robust oak were used to build a ship in Nelson's time — the Victory took six years to complete, and in 1805 a 74-gun ship of the line required 2,500 tons of timber sawn and carved from perhaps 700 large oak growing on up to 60 acres of land.

Most conifers adapt well to poorer, shallower soils found on many hillsides within the parish. And there is a place for deciduous species under these conditions — for amenity and conservation consideration, (9% of the forest area is occupied by broadleaved trees), but not as a competitive commercial forest crop. After all much of the timber felled around Betws-y-coed between 1914-18 had been close to 200 years old; it had not been managed as a commercial venture and was growing in an age when industrial demands were nowhere near as critical, competitive and voracious as they are to-day.

What one sees now around Betws-y-coed is representative of the Forestry Commission's objectives and achievements since the early plantings of the 1920's. The forest landscape cannot be conserved by arresting growth at a particular moment in time. Subtle variations are continuously taking place and effective forest management creates a cycle of change, beginning with new plantations and changing slowly as the trees grow older and are thinned. The crop is harvested when it achieves economic maturity — the impact on the landscape can then be sudden, dramatic and total; but just as new tree planting must reflect the natural diversity of the soil, aspect and the landform itself, so felling can be designed to coincide with natural boundaries and features. Preserving the visual harmony of the landscape is well illustrated in the woodlands around the village.

When we consider the momentum and diversity of modern life, the Victorians, if they could return, one feels sure, would not be offended by the wooded appearance on the hillsides round Betws-y-coed to-day.

Three generations of some families living in the village have found employment in Gwydir forest, but only a handful of the smallholdings remain in occupation. The largest timber is sold to sawmills in Conwy or along the English border; smaller material is sold for pulp to Shotton or to Chirk for chipboard. Fencing stakes are also produced.

Gwydir forest occupies 14,900 acres or 23 square miles, with 5990 acres under plantations. 138 miles of road have been constructed, and by 1990 the forecast volume of timber available for produce is 48,000 cubic metres.

There are many forest walks available to the public, and brochures and other information may be obtained at the Visitor Information Centre in the village.

GWYDYR HOTEL

Until a few years ago, this hotel was managed by the same family for over 100 years. One of Betws-y-coed's hotels with a long and prudent reputation, the Gwydyr has been associated with angling and fishery know-how for many decades (See Angling). The hotel owns stretches of the Conwy and Lledr and these offer fine prospects for catching good sized fish when conditions are right. Permits and information are available at the hotel.

During the times of horse-drawn coaches this hostlery took passengers to local places of interest — Swallow Falls, Fairy Glen, etc in a two-horse wagonette. In 1877, when income tax was two pence (.85p) in the £, the hotel could purchase 48 lbs of prime Scotch beef for a gold sovereign (£1) and a housemaid would work contentedly for £10 a year and her keep.

During the 1920's the hotel owned a large restaurant (complete with Chinese lanterns), tennis courts and a bowling green on the site where the caravan park is now situated.

GYPSIES

For some six weeks during the summer throughout the 1930's, three to four caravans with gypsy families used to arrive and halt by the roadside at Waterloo spinney, behind the hotel.

They would make baskets from osier, a species of willow, and go around the village selling them; they also made pegs, at times biding their opportunity and wandering into people's gardens and severing the occasional ash branch, and a few days later, returning and selling pegs made from those same branches to the householder at twelve pegs for sixpence.

They kept themselves clean, left not a speck of litter where they had stayed, and were appreciated for their help at railway fires and lending a hand at haymaking time on some of the local farms.

H

HACKNEY CARRIAGES

At the first meeting of Betws-y-coed Urban District Council in 1898 it was resolved that appointment to the post of Inspector of Hackney carriages should carry a salary of £3 a year. The appointment was to be made for one year in the first instance and subject to the approval of the Local Government Board.

In 1899 the Betws-y-coed council issued a total of 27 carriages and drivers' licenses to local applicants.

HAFOD AND HENDRE

Hafod means a summer dwelling and Hendre signifies a sheltered winter habitation, and within the village are two properties associated with the meaning of these words. They illustrate the situation and example of dwellings that in past days typified a way of life that involved the migration for a few months of the resident families and all their livestock.

The first property is Hendre Rhys Gethin, once a farm, situated some 100 feet above sea level in a sheltered location just off the A5, a ½ mile or so west of Pont-y-pair. The other is Hafodlas, once an upland farm close to Llyn Elsi and Hafodlas quarry and located nearly 700 ft above, and slightly west of, Hendre Rhys Gethin. Both properties are occupied now but the occupants are no longer engaged in agricultural practices.

The upland areas around Betws-y-coed are not really

Hendre Rhys Gethin

suitable for land cultivation — being too rocky and ridged —
and so the tending of livestock rather than tillage prevailed for
centuries.

Prior to the Enclosure acts a seasonal movement or
migration of all local livestock took place around the end of
May from the sheltered lowland farmsteads (the Hendre) to
the summer mountain unit (the Hafod) where livestock would
be free to graze throughout the warmer months. This
migration would more often than not include the whole
family, household goods, chattels, provisions, dogs, cats,
poultry, pigs and goats. It would have been a mass exodus,
with sleds and carts in use, and cattle and sheep driven on
ahead. Once in the uplands, milking was done out of doors
and the grazing cattle, goats and sheep tended from dawn to
dusk.

With the approach of Autumn the movement became
reversed and the whole household and their livestock
returned to the warmth and shelter of the Hendre. This
migration to the hills ceased as an annual occurrence around

about 1860. One part of Hafodlas showed evidence of pre-15th century construction. It was during the period of Owain Glyndŵr's rebellion in 1400, when he and his followers plundered much of the Conwy valley and King Henry IV, in retaliation, decreed that among other penalties, "no Welshman was to build a house higher than one in which the rafters on each side were to reach the ground". In other words every Welshman must erect his house without any side walls.

A property of that description would prove to be quite unmanageable, but, "as a carriage and four can be driven through any statute", so the wily Welshmen found the means to evade this harsh enactment without exactly defying and breaking it. When building was about to begin, a search would be made in the woods for any crooked trees, the bends of which had to be strong enough to form rafters, and the upright part naturally came to the ground. These rafters were set at a proper distance from each other and stone walls were then built on each side to reach the bends. By this method people in the olden days provided comfortable tenement without breaking the law.

HAFODLAS QUARRY

This modest sized quarry, located between 400-500 ft above sea level along the hillside above Pentre-Du, used to produce 2,000 tons of roofing slate a year.

These slates underly the lowest local sandstone and include a tuffaceous band composed of white mica and much altered crystals of feldspar. The product was brought down the hillside by trams running on a narrow-gauge track down an incline and controlled by a rope-worked pulley system.

The working periods of small local quarries such as this coincided with two developing interests — the railways who called out for slate for roofing their stations and for the provision of window ledges, and the expanding number of hotels and boarding houses being built along the N. Wales coast and all requiring roofing slate.

Some of the slate was taken to a wharf at Trefriw and shipped from there along with lead ore, timber, bark and corn. A slate merchant who had dealings with Hafodlas

Pentre Du and Hafodlas Quarry tips on the left

quarry and other small quarries at Dolwyddelan and Penmachno, used to ship 47 tons a week of local slate, and because of its quality and reputation for withstanding heat, it was exported to places as far afield as New Orleans.

A whole street of houses (Gethin Terrace) was built at Pentre Du, at the west end of Betws-y-coed, towards the close of the 19th century, so that quarry workmen and their families would be domiciled near to the place of work. Remains of this quarry may be seen among the trees above Pentre-Du, and a track to Llyn Elsi passes close to one of the spoil tips. Every care should be taken not to dislodge debris on any of these tips, and it is unwise to penetrate any tunnels or scramble around old buildings.

HORSE TROUGH

Erected in 1888 and sited between the Post Office and St Mary's Church, this trough commemorates those faraway days when horse-drawn omnibuses served the village and surrounding district. It was presented to the village at the time when a Llandudno businessman was advertising four-in-hand excursions to Swallow Falls and Snowdonia. Some of the coaches were uniquely named — "The Rocket", "Old Times" etc. The fare from Llandudno to Swallow Falls was seven shillings (35p). A larger coach "The Prince of Wales" took passengers into Snowdonia, leaving Llandudno at 8.45am and arriving at Betws-y-coed for lunch at 11.15.

HORSESHOE IN A TREE

At the side of the by-road that passes through Diosgydd woods — a route many visitors take to view the Swallow Falls — there stood at one time the remains of an old oak tree trunk with a horseshoe embedded in it about five feet from the ground. This horseshoe was enclosed so firmly that it couldn't be moved or prised away, and local folk were unsure as to its origin. One theory was that, years back, a local farmer's horse had shed its shoe and the owner had picked it up and placed it in a crotch between the trunk and a side branch. He never returned to claim it. Many years passed and the outer bark slowly grew round the horseshoe, almost enclosing it.

On a hot Whitsun day in the mid-1930's a visitor was standing looking at the horseshoe and writing in a notebook, when a forest patrolman came along. They conversed for several minutes about the mysterious horseshoe and how strong and durable tree growth could be. Before parting, the visitor — a Lancastrian — handed the patrolman a page from his notebook on which he had written four lines.

When his tour of duty had finished the patrolman called at the Head Forester's house and handed the page to him. The quotation read:

> "Pretty! in amber, to observe the forms
> Of hairs, or straws, or dirt, or grubs, or worms.
> The things, we know, are neither rich nor rare,
> But wonder how the devil they got there!"

Whoever he was, Alexander Pope was no stranger to this scholarly Lancastrian!

I

ICE FLOES

During the severe winter of 1963 ice floes were observed in the Conwy river for the first time in living memory.

INFORMATION CENTRE

This Visitor Information Centre was at one time the stable buildings belonging to the Royal Oak Hotel. It was here that pupils of Dulwich College Prep School had some classrooms when they were evacuated to the village in 1940. At one time nine cottages and a tavern stood on this site. A policeman was resident in one of the cottages, and behind it a small lock-up had been erected. Petty summonses against the law were dealt with in one of the other cottages, and for those persons committing misdemeanours, a stock was in position close to the present arch entrance.

IRON-AGED HILLTOP ENCLOSURE

Listed as an early Iron-Aged Fort (600BC-100AD), it is more likely that this iron-aged feature was a defended hilltop enclosure. The knoll on which it is located is 800 ft above sea level (100 ft higher than the prominent crag known as Clogwyn Dinas, which is just over ½ mile away to the SW.) Not much evidence can be seen to-day, but a number of large boulders present the appearance of having been assigned to positions affording the best defence, and a depression, which may have given cover, is quite evident.

The rocky knoll on which the enclosure is situated rises above the former smallholding (tyddyn) known as Tan-y-Castell (Under the Castle) — now a private residence — about one mile NW of Betws-y-coed.

The track to Coedmawr and Llyn Sarnau passes beneath this knoll and was, not all that long ago, recognised as a Council-maintained route.

Quite probably, away back in time, this could have been a Roman route from the south at Miner's Bridge, where Sarn Helen comes down to the A5, and proceeding north across a causeway at llyn Sarnau and carrying on above Trefriw to Pen-y-Gaer.

The old lead mine known as Coedmawr Pool is very close to this track and the probability is that some speculative mining was undertaken by the Romans. As John Williams in his book Faunula Grustensis, published in 1830, recorded, "Lead mines abound in this place and have been dug for ages, as there have been many relics found which proved that the Romans explored the bowels of the Nant".

ITINERARY IN WALES (1536-39)

This guide was written by John Leland, that estimable antiquarian and chronicler of the 16th century, who declared that the best wood in N. Wales was seen between Capel Curig and the Lledr valley and would almost, without doubt, include the hillsides around Betws-y-coed.

J

JEX-BLAKE, SOPHIA

The population of Betws-y-coed was 451 in 1847, and forty scholars attended lessons in a cottage under the instruction of one master who had no educational qualifications whatsoever, and who worked in the village as a craftsman. The fees were a penny a week.

A few years later village education took a dramatic upward turn through the interest and concern of a remarkable woman — Sophia Jex-Blake, who became Britain's first woman physician. A frequent visitor to Betws-y-coed, whose beauty she admired so much, she became aware of the poor educational facilities available to scholars in the village. Miss Jex-Blake resolved to improve them, and in 1858, on her annual holiday, she gave a few lessons to children on various subjects.

The next step was to acquire a plot of land on which to endow a purpose-built school, the first in the village. Lord Willoughby de Eresby provided this — adjacent to the A5, on the site where the imposing Gallery building now stands, and arrangements were made to supply the builders with stone from Hafodlas quarry. Farmers voluntarily carried this down in carts free of charge, and Miss Jex-Blake had her school completed by 1869.

She founded the London School of Medicine for Women in 1874, and her visits to her beloved Betws-y-coed continued year after year until early this century.

JONES, BEN — RHIWGRI

Undergrowth and ivy have now practically invaded the ruins of this pleasantly situated tyddyn (or smallholding), but it may still be seen to-day at the side of a forest road and reached by a walk leading up from St Mary's Church and described in Forest Walk 1. (Obtainable at the Visitor Information Centre). (See also RHYS OF THE COCKS).

The last occupant was an elderly bachelor, Ben Jones, who was employed by the Forestry Commission and spent much of his time cleaning out ditches among young plantations to ensure a free flow of water.

A farm census undertaken in 1938 reveals that Ben Jones kept 64 sheep on 76 acres of 'ffridd' (mountain pasture) which went with his smallholding. Much of the land has been planted, but stone walls which divided the grazings, and the odd small outbuilding, can still be observed to-day among the trees.

Ben lived in Rhiwgri until the 1940's and is remembered by some who knew him for his pet cockerel. This followed him everywhere — into the forest, out to the pastures when he inspected his sheep and down to the village when he made his weekly visit for provisions. It even followed him into the tap room of a local hostlery and crouched, alert and quite at home, under a bench while Ben consumed his ale.

However there was an altercation one summer evening between Ben and the landlady and he was told to get off home and take his cockerel with him. At the time Ben was clearly a mite tipsy and he found it difficult to get his cockerel into a canvas bag he sometimes used to carry it around in. Tying up the neck and throwing the bag over his shoulder he staggered off up the hill homewards, but before he got to Rhiwgri his legs gave out. He fell asleep snoring on a grassy bank and around dawn, when he awoke, the first thing he became aware of was the sight of a writhing sack a few feet away, from which a raucous squaking was issuing. Thoroughly alarmed, Ben scrambled to his feet and fled homewards and it wasn't until he reached his front door that he realised it was his pet cockerel that was imprisoned in the sack. Muttering imprecations he set off back down the track to retrieve it and release his pet.

Ben recounted this incident to a colleague a day or so later when they were working in the woods. His cockerel survived the ordeal without harm, but thereafter Ben Jones was wary of taking it with him on his weekly excursions down to the village.

"JUBILEE" PATHS

There are two popular and long established walks following these paths. Both pass through hillsides rich in history, and culminate in spectacular vistas.

The first of these, and the shortest, begins a short distance from Pont-y-pair car park (where the route is indicated on a map). There are a few short, steep pitches as one ascends from 200 to 600 ft and arrives at the summit — Clogwyn Cyrau. From here there are fine views across the village and valley.

The second Jubilee Path can be found by going up a short flight of stone steps close by the Cross Keys restaurant, some 400 yards along the A5 from Pont-y-pair.

This path winds through the plantations of Fedw Hendre and in one section overlooks the old Gwydir deciduous woods behind St Mary's Church. Hafodlas quarry may also be glimpsed as the final stage is reached — and there, complete with its small, rocky isles dotted on its waters, is Llyn Elsi.

JUDGES

This well-known firm of photographic publishers, with their extensive range of postcards covering many local scenes around the village, owned premises next to Betws-y-coed Post Office for very many years.

Their stock of postcards included many sepia scenes around Betws-y-coed from 1910 to 1920/21.

Apart from selling a miscellany of postcards and writing materials, Judges also kept a well patronized lending library on the premises. The company sold out to a local businessman a few years ago.

JUKES, JOSEPH B.

J. B. Jukes was a member of a geological team undertaking work in the complicated geological area north-west of Betws-y-coed in 1850.

About the time of year he was engaged with his survey work the village hotels and guest houses were full to their attics with visitors, and Jukes complained bitterly about the lack of adequate accommodation and the unreasonable charges for food.

"These confounded artists," he wrote, "won't go away. I'm almost reduced to a standstill, every house is crammed full of amateurs of scenery and salmon fishers!"

Little further proof of the village's popularity is really necessary, except for the observations of a frustrated member of one professional body at least!

K

KNIGHT, JOSEPH

Minafon (brink or side of the river) is situated close to Waterloo bridge, on the by-lane leading to Craig-y-Dderwen

Country House Hotel.

It was built about 1879 by a much respected artist — the one-armed Joseph Knight — renowned for his mezzo-tint engravings. Knight, who had a great affection for Betws-y-coed, lived at Minafon for many years before retiring to Chelsea. Another artist, George Harrison, leased the property and lived there until 1910.

It was then bought by a Doctor Porritt and subsequently occupied by a succession of medical practitioners — Doctors Waller, Milne and Bowden. An excellent artist's studio was used as a surgery.

A very recent village practitioner, Dr Chown, has now retired there.

KURTZ, CHARLES

The property known as Coed-y-Celyn (Wood of Holly) lies alongside the A470, about ½ mile east of Waterloo bridge and close to Fairy Glen, Beaver Bridge and Beaver Pool.

Charles Kurtz, a Pole, who owned a chemical business in Liverpool, was the original owner who only part completed building the property before he died. His estate fell into Chancery and eventually, when his children all reached 21, the property was sold after being empty for many years. Later it was renovated and extended and was at one time a private hotel. To-day the first floor has been divided into flats, but most of the ground floor is owned by one family, the resident occupants being founder members of the Celyn Music Society. The music room at Coed-y-Celyn is used for a series of concerts held during the winter months.

L

LLEDR BRIDGE (PONT AR LLEDR)

About ⅓ of a mile upriver of Beaver bridge, and opposite Ivy Glen house beside the A470 to Dolwyddelan, this wonderful old bridge across the Lledr is one of the lesser known attractions of Betws-y-coed. It certainly doesn't deserve to be, for if one just pauses for a while by the bridge in its setting among trees, its unique presence seems to convey one back to another age in time. Perhaps it should give this impression, for it was built at the latter end of the 15th century and is made up of two elliptical arches — the larger one spans the river, the smaller one absorbs any floodwater after heavy rainfall has increased the volume.

Between this bridge and Beaver bridge are the remains of an old tollgate by the side of the A470, with a bench mark with the figures 87.12.

LLEDR RIVER (AFON LLEDR)

This river rises close to the Crimea Pass, above Blaenau Ffestiniog, winds past Dolwyddelan, and threads its course through Lledr valley until it meets with the Conwy at Cymer Afon (river confluence), just above Beaver bridge.

The valley of the Lledr is widely acclaimed as being one of the most attractive in the country. Rail, road and river are embraced within its rocky hillsides and terraces and tree-clad bluffs. Truly a valley of great character, and seen at its best when autumnal tints prosper, and clothe the rugged hillsides in luminous shades from amber to russet and gold.

LLUGWY RIVER (AFON LLUGWY)

The eminent Welsh scholar, Sir Ifor Williams, considered that the root of the word 'Llugwy' might be Welsh for bright — an allusion perhaps to the river's numerous shimmering rapids and foaming cascades. Some of the rapids are shallow, others deep.

Source of Afon Llugwy is in a high, remote lake called Ffynnon Llugwy (1786 ft) deep in the Carneddau range. It then descends to Capel Curig and over its first major falls at Cyffyng, on then under Tŷ Hyll bridge and into the Llugwy valley proper via Swallow Falls, Miners' Bridge falls and Pont-y-pair. Its turbulence seemingly satisfied, its waters curl rather more gently round between Mill Street and the Visitor Centre and join the Conwy about one third of a mile to the north, at the extremity of the golf course.

Moel Siabod from Llidiart y Gwynt

The "Meeting of the Waters" — the confluence of the Llugwy and Conwy rivers near Betws-y-coed

Geologists use the term 'nick points' or notches and point out that these can be well observed at waterfalls and rapids on the Llugwy — Pont-y-pair, the falls upriver of Miners' Bridge, Swallow Falls and Cyffyng Falls.

Before they were breached, these obstacles would have held the meltwater in small lakes, and it is possible that the alluvial flats now seen on their upstream side, were, in part, lacustrine (dwelling or growing in lakes). Other 'nick points' are present in the Conwy and Lledr rivers.

Vistas are not so prominent in the Llugwy valley as they are in the Lledr; woodland clothes the slopes from near Tŷ Hyll to Miners' Bridge and many natural features are obscured, and will remain so until the trees are thinned or felled. On the northern side of the river the prominent crag known as 'Summerhouse Crag' overlooks the Swallow Falls. About the middle of the 1920's the walls of this building were demolished as it was considered they were unsafe, and the summerhouse had not been in use for many years. Local historians believe that many years ago there was some association between this structure and the old manor house at Pencraig, about a ½ mile away, and there was even speculation about a secret tunnel connecting the two places.

Moel Siabod (2860ft) dominates the landscape at Capel Curig but cannot be seen from the confines of the middle and lower reaches of the valley.

The A5 route parallels the river until they part company at Betws-y-coed.

LLWYD, ELLEN

Ellen Llwyd, a well known local character of last century, was the wife of the village cobbler, David Llwyd. They lived in a small cottage close to the Royal Oak hotel and Ellen would often sit outside the cottage dressed in national costume. Frequently, in the summer, she would entertain guests in the hotel after the evening meal with folk dancing which she'd learned as a young girl, and with recitations.

When her daughter married and went to live in London, old Ellen used to visit her as often as possible and by all accounts thoroughly enjoyed her time in the capital. She seemed to have developed a fondness for London gin and on occasions, as the consequence of a merry 'tipple', she set off doing a folk dance along the Strand, fortunately without causing a brush with the law!

M

MAMMALS

The principal mammals to be observed within the Betws-y-coed parish are:-

SPECIES	STATUS	LOCATION
Hedgehog	Fairly common	Thickets; mixed woodland; some hedgerows; sheltered positions.
Mole	Common	Fields and meadowland. Banks — and sometimes un unwelcome visitor to one's garden!
Mountain Hare (See comment below)	Quite rare	Uplands above 600 ft.
Rabbit	Increasing in some localities since Myxomatosis first appeared	Pastures; banks near to thickets; light woodland.
Red Squirrel	Very rare. Some rufous-coloured individuals observed in pine areas on high ground.	Pine woods on higher elevations.

Grey Squirrel	Fairly common	Conifer plantations; copses; some mixed woodland areas.
Otter	Extremely rare	not being divulged.
Pine Marten	Extremely rare	not being divulged.
Polecat	Locally numbers are increasing	Stone walls; old tree stumps;
Stoat	Fairly common	Boulder-strewn ground; rocky places; walls; rough pasture.
Weasel	Locally common	Holes in banks, walls;
Badger	Very local	not being divulged
Fox	Quite common	Plantations and rocky cover.

Comment on Mountain Hare by Fred Owen, ex-Forestry Commission trapper. This well known local trapper was once asked if the mountain hare provided good meat, and what was the best method of cooking it. Fred's sceptical reply was: "The best method of cooking a mountain hare? Just follow this recipe an' you won't go wrong, aye; you boil the hare with one of the oldest boots you can find n'aye. Keep on boilin' the two together an' when the boot is soft an' tender you throw the -------- hare away and eat the boot."

MEAN MONTHLY TEMPERATURES AT BETWS-Y-COED (°F)

January	39.8
February	40.3
March	41.8
April	45.9
May	51.0
June	56.4
July	58.8
August	58.3
September	54.8

October	48.6
November	43.5
December	41.0

Average for year – 48.4

MAURICE AB HUGH

The remains of this much respected man lay in St Michael's churchyard under a flat, grey stone bearing the following inscription — "Here lyeth the body of the late ingenious Maurice ab Hugh, who was buried the 24th day of October, 1735, aged 66".

It appears that this man, a bachelor, was a blacksmith in the village, and possessed some secret means of welding steel and other metals in such a way as to defy discovery of the join. Old women brought him their broken darning and knitting needles and he repaired them without difficulty.

One summer day a gentleman appeared in the village in considerable agitation, having fallen and broken his favourite sword while scrambling in the woods searching for Dafydd ap Siencyn's cave on Carreg Gwalch, above Gwydir Castle. His sword had accompanied him in campaigns fought under William III and the first Duke of Marlborough, and he was distressed at the thought of losing so valuable a weapon.

A resident informed him of the blacksmith's skill at repairing metals, and despite being somewhat sceptical at this information the man approached the smith and begged him to see if he could repair his sword. Maurice ab Hugh took the two halves, examined them carefully and went into his workroom. The stranger made to follow him but was waved away and told to wait outside. No one was going to spy on the smith at his work!

Within a short time and to his great joy and astonishment the sword was returned to him complete and with no visible indication of where the two halves had been joined.

The gentleman's name was Captain Robert Wynn, descended in the same line from Owen Gwynedd as the Wynns of Gwydir. He showed his gratitude to Maurice ab Hugh in a substantial manner and on the blacksmith's death made the arrangements for placing the stone with the inscription on it over his final resting place.

MILL STREET

The B5106 road to Gwydir Castle follows this street which leads off from Pont-y-pair bridge. The street once contained two inns and is reputedly one of the earliest locations in the village to have been permanently inhabited.

The quaint house on the left bank next to the Memorial Hall is known as Bryn-y-bont, but little is known of its history.

Mill Street derives its name from the old corn mill situated about ½ way down the street on the left. Little remains to-day of the mill which ceased working in 1940. Excellent oat cakes were made from grain locally grown and ground.

The mill wheel was turned by water which was directed from Afon Llugwy just below Still Pool, and controlled by a sluice gate into a leat passing beneath the road where the car

Mill Street, Betws-y-coed

park is now located, and then led, uncovered, to the rear of the mill. A conduit beneath Mill Street led the tailrace of water away from the mill into Afon Llugwy.

The village surgery and car park are, to-day, located on the right hand side at the northern end of the street.

MINERS' BRIDGE

One of Betws-y-coed's popular sights, this bridge spans the Llugwy at a narrow point a mile upstream from Pont-y-pair.

It is conceivable that somewhere close by, the very first crossing of the Llugwy was made, as the Roman road Sarn Helen, emerges from the south barely a hundred yards away, and in all probability a ford below the present bridge allowed the route to continue along an ancient track northward to Pen-y-gaer.

The first bridge may only have been a couple of tree trunks slung across the river, but as the lead mines to the north expanded in the latter half of last century and work was available for the men from Pentre Du, a more permanent structure was erected.

To-day's bridge takes the form of a gangway. Upstream is a rather gloomy looking pool, Pwll Du (Black Pool), and beyond it an attractive waterfalls with the odd pothole scoured out of the rocks.

Between 1914-18 a sawmill was in operation in the woods behind the top end of the bridge, converting trees felled on the hillside above into the required lengths.

MOTHS

The active lepidopterist F. D. Bland found moths of all the main families were quite plentiful around Betws-y-coed in 1899. Many still are, including the Yellow Underwing, Golden-Rod-Brindle and Light Knotgrass, all three being moorland moths.

Of considerable local interest was a moth first found in the vicinity of Betws-y-coed in 1855 and named "Sterrha Eburnata" (Weaver's Wave).

Miners' Bridge over Llugwy River

1934 RILEY MPH

MOTOR MUSEUM

To the rear of the Information Centre, this museum with its collection of vintage and post-vintage thoroughbred cars, is contained within some of the buildings that once constituted Royal Oak Farm. The Thomases were the last family to occupy the premises when it was still a farm — and apart from that occupation, two or three of the sons supplied coal to some of the villagers and had a haulage business as well. They also had a contract to collect and dispose of refuse.

The museum buildings have been carefully and attractively designed to harmonize with the character of the old farm fabric.

Across the lane which leads to the meeting of the waters — the rivers Conwy and Llugwy — is the old Royal Oak, farmhouse, now a private dwelling. The remnants of a leat leading from the Llugwy to the old farmhouse can still be seen; this led water to turn an undershot water wheel. No one recalls seeing it work, but its purpose was to supply mechanical power to the Royal Oak farm for agricultural use, including the churning of large quantities of milk to supply visitors with fresh butter.

MYXOMATOSIS

This offensive disease affecting rabbits was first reported within the vicinity of the village in 1954.

N

NANT CONWY AND NANT CONWY HUNDREDS

The whole of the Conwy valley, including Betws-y-coed, was laid waste by Edward the Fourth in 1468 during the Wars of the Roses. He sent a large army under the Earl of Pembroke to pillage and destroy, and the outcome was a huge success for the Yorkists. For the stricken survivors their fate was lamented in these lines —

> "But poor Nant Conwy suffered more,
> For there the flames burnt higher.
> 'Twas in the year of our Lord,
> Fourteen Hundred Sixty-eight,
> That these unhappy parts of Wales
> Met with such a wretched fate".

In 1536, Betws-y-coed comprised one of five parishes within the Nant Conwy Hundreds, and the district at that time came under the jurisdiction of Sir John Wynn of Gwydir.

NINETEEN HUNDRED (1900)

In 1900 the Clerk's salary was £25 per annum; the General District Rates were 2/3 (10.3p) in the £; the Solicitor to the Council, when appointed, was paid a retaining fee of £3.3.0 (£3.15p) for one year, plus scale charges in the event of litigation or extraordinary business.

The Medical Officer's Report for 1900 indicated the area of the parish to be 3,636 acres, the population to be 740 and the annual death rate was 19.8.

O

"OLD TIMES"

In 1900 this was the name of a coach owned by a Mr Harley of Llandudno. It was kept at the Gwydir hotel where it carried culinary items back and forth between Betws-y-coed and Llandudno, and during the tourist season it transported residents to Swallow Falls and Fairy Glen.

ORCHIDS

An extensive family and well distributed all over the world, some selected species of orchid are to be found within the Parish of Betws-y-coed. The species growing in this country are terrestrial, though a large proportion of the tropical ones are epiphytes, growing upon tree stems, but without penetrating the tissues.

Of those found around Betws-y-coed, Twayblade grows best in moist pasture and woods and flowers both in spring and summer; Spotted Orchis and Early Purple Orchis can be found in meadows and moist open woods. The Fragrant Orchis flowers all summer, and as its name implies, the flowers are sweet-scented. Butterfly Orchis has pure white flowers or with a slight greenish tinge, and is also sweet-scented.

OWEN, FRED — THE GAMEKEEPER WHO HID BEER BOTTLES

In the decade when Prohibition dominated American society, and Alexander Fleming discovered penicillin, Frederick Charles Owen was appointed to the post of official trapper at Gwydir forest. His responsibilities were clearly defined — the elimination of large rabbit populations from all land taken in hand for planting each year and the control of sheep trespass in young plantations.

An ex-cavalryman of stocky, powerful build, Fred lived with his wife Kate at Tan Dinas, a favourably located boarding house on the outskirts of Betws-y-coed. His first trio of dogs held no respectable pedigree at all. (Later he would obtain well-bred Springer spaniels), — they were just three tousled canines, a sheepdog, a terrier and a cocker spaniel who tackled the rough hillside terrain, the dense gorse cover and bramble thickets day in day out, month on month, year after year with stout hearts and rare stamina until eventually they were retired from active work. Fred would follow his dogs on the chase, urging them on, scrambling across scree slopes, along ledges and terraces, calling, whistling, encouraging — a D'Artagnan to his three faithful canine musketeers. Shooting the quarry against a backcloth of grey scree or speckled vegetation called for a high degree of accuracy and Fred was a fine shot. He was never known to leave a wounded animal to linger painfully and die.

Locally everyone knew him as "Owen keeper", and with his dogs strung out behind him he became as familiar a figure as the police sargeant or the local minister as he trudged through Betws-y-coed on his way to plantations on the rocky hillsides. He had to keep note of the number of rabbits he killed each week and hand in their tails to a foreman; he could dispose of the rabbits as he wished. Some he sold to hotels and a number Fred gave away to deserving folk. On many an occasion an elderly resident or a widow with children would open their door of a morning and find a rabbit, sometimes two, neatly gutted and skinned, wrapped in paper and laid upon the doorstep. Only rarely did they glimpse the familiar figure of the trapper leaving the premises in the cold, grey morning light. But Fred Owen had an Achilles heel — a fondness for ale. It got him into trouble with his employers during his early years of service because he would keep nipping into public houses during working hours. An intake of beer seemed an essential ingredient, as though it restored verve after many weary hours spent scrambling around on the hillsides. Fred couldn't resist it. Never did he become wildly inebriated or give way to angry outbursts or profanity, and he'd never been known to be disorderly or give offence. Kate, his wife, was well aware of his Achilles heel — it made not the slightest difference to the affection or rapport between them.

Eventually Betws-y-coed was declared out of bounds to Fred Owen during working hours. He was ordered to control himself or the consequences would be final and no one would be more sorry to see Fred dismissed than his Head Forester. Fred did put his house in order during working hours and kept strictly away from the village hostleries. But on Saturday nights he'd go down to Pont-y-pair hotel, imbibe a pint or two of ale and purchase a half-dozen pint bottles of beer to take home. The following Monday he'd pack these bottles in a haversack, carry it into the forest and thrust the bottles down the entrances to old rabbit warrens or beneath clumps of gorse or under shelving rocks. He'd repeat this practice week after week until there were dozens of bottles distributed over parts of the forest and whose contents awaited consumption at Fred's pleasure.

All very well — but it was easy to forget where exactly they were located as time passed. After all there were scores of rabbit holes and gorse clumps and shelving rocks all over the forest. Assuredly Fred succeeded in recovering many and enjoyed the contents, but long after he'd retired forest folk would come upon an unopened pint beer bottle in an ancient rabbit burrow or under a patch of gorse. Sure evidence that Fred Owen had long ago overlooked their location. By tradition Fred duly planted a tree in Artist's wood on his retirement after over thirty years service. Where once he'd trapped rabbits on sunlit open spaces or grass banks, now tall trees grew in proud dignity. He'd covered hundreds of miles across some of the roughest terrain in Wales, fought many a forest fire and rescued stray sheep trapped on ledges and on rocks in the middle of mountain streams swollen by heavy rain. And he'd survived all these experiences without injury.

Once, as he approached retirement and was in bed with a heavy chill, the local undertaker called to see if his weekly order for a rabbit was available. Kate Owen explained the circumstances and asked him to call again in a few day's time. The undertaker retired meekly, tending his sincere wish that Fred might soon recover. When he was informed of the caller's identity, Fred couldn't resist a gibe.

"Kate, if he calls again show him up" he croaked." If I'm alive I'll be pleased to see the old devil and if I'm dead there's little doubt he'll be pleased to see me".

There is little doubt that there will be a corner of Gwydir forest that will be forever Fred Owen — and one suspects, quite close to an ancient rabbit burrow or beneath a dense cover of gorse.

Pencraig today

OWEN, WILLIAM (PENCRAIG)

During the late 17th century William Owen, the owner of
Pencraig, a farm and small estate slightly to the west of the
Betws-y-coed parish boundary, was a widely known and much
respected bard and harpist, who, by some misdeed or other
incurred the displeasure of the King. The sentence of
outlawry was passed on him and two officers of the law were
despatched to arrest him. Owen was performing upon the
triple harp at a meeting of the bards in Conwy when he had
news of his imminent arrest, and a shipowner friend of his
prevailed upon him to board his vessel in the harbour and
escape to Flanders.

Owen concurred at once and fled the town in such haste that
he left no word of his whereabouts at either Betws-y-coed or
Pencraig. His wife gave up all hope of his return and
considered herself justified in looking for a fresh partner for

protection in life. And after fifteen years she became betrothed to the man acting as a bailiff in the management of the land at Pencraig.

The wedding day was announced and late in the evening prior to the wedding an old soldier put in an appearance at an inn in Betws-y-coed, and after some refreshment made enquiries of the innkeeper as to who lived at Pencraig. The innkeeper, who did not recognise him, replied that a Mrs Owen resided there and because her husband had been outlawed years ago and believed to have been killed in the French wars, she was to be married on the morrow.

The old soldier left and made his way to Pencraig. Humbly knocking at the door he enquired for lodging for the night — he was a poor bard and harpist he explained. His request was granted and after supper he expressed a wish to amuse his hosts by playing some tunes on a harp if they would let him.

There was only one harp in the house someone told him — the old one belonging to William Owen — and no one could play it as the owner had taken the tuning key with him when he went absent. The guest persisted in his request however and at length the harp was brought to him reluctantly and he was told that better minstrels than he appeared to be had failed to play a tune on it.

Quietly drawing a key from his pocket and caressing the strings of his favourite old instrument he began playing a long lost tune composed by William Owen and known as the 'Conceit of William Owen, Pencraig'. The intimacy of this tune and the manner in which it was played convinced the company that he must be the long lost husband returned again, but Mrs Owen was not totally convinced until she scanned one of his ears carefully and found thereon a scar caused years before by the bite of a dog.

That completely satisfied her! The whole house was in commotion and in the midst of all the excitement the would-be bridegroom slipped out and fled down the road as fast as his legs would carry him. He was never heard from again, and William Owen, reunited with his family, lived on contentedly at Pencraig for many more years.

OXFAM WALKS

With the co-operation of the Forestry Commission, the Bangor branch of Oxfam arranged a series of sponsored walks (length 26 miles) to raise funds for its charitable institutions. The first walk was held in 1972, when 800 walkers participated and £3,500 was raised. The start — at 10am — was at the Betws-y-coed station forecourt, and participants then followed a series of internal roads through Gwydir forest, and completed the course at the Memorial Hall, Betws-y-coed, where they 'signed off'.

The forest route was a scenic one with two refreshment and rest stations — and, most importantly, held no danger or interference from traffic.

The first walk was so successful that it became an annual event for several years after, and more and more participants took part from all over North Wales. The Red Cross were always in attendance to minister to blistered feet and soothe anguished brows, and forest personnel saw to it that no one strayed from the well-identified route.

P

PARC LAKE (LLYN PARC)

Nearly 700 ft above sea level, this narrow lake — well over ½ a mile in length — has a contracted waist near its centre, and it was at this point that flames from the great forest fire of May 1938 jumped the lake from west to east and spread fiercely through much of the High Parc area (See Forest fires).

The mill at Aberllyn mine was powered by a turbine driven by water from Parc lake and levels from the mine were once driven beneath parts of the lake.

Gorse had always grown vigorously in High Parc, and in times gone by it had contributed considerably to horse feed. When tree growth was sparse over the area, the gorse crop was cut by the Gwydir estate staff when still young and succulent and carried down to a silo at Gwydir Uchaf for conversion to silage. The estate used to treat the area on a selective gorse

Llyn Parc

cycle, cutting so many acres one year, moving on to an adjacent site the next, and returning perhaps in 2-3 years time to the initial cutting area. The Wynn family were ardent horse lovers and Lady Mary Wynn favoured a bridle path which led up through the woods to Llanrychwyn and the church there.

At one time the area around Parc lake was enclosed by a seven-foot high drystone wall, part built by French prisoners during the Napoleonic wars. Sections may still be seen to-day, and a herd of deer roamed this enclosed area until about the end of last century.

The waters are too toxic to support a fish population, due to an outflow from a lead mine adit at the north end of the lake.

On the western edge, a wood of mainly mixed deciduous trees contributes an attractive contrast along the surrounds of this peaceful upland lake.

PEARLS

When he was treasurer to Henrietta Maria, Queen of Charles

1st, Sir Richard Wynn of Gwydir presented her Majesty with a pearl from the river Conwy to adorn the Royal Crown.

Centuries later the presence of pearls in the local rivers was confirmed by Canon R. Williams in his 'History of Aberconwy' (1835). Furthermore, the Canon declared that the river Conwy, in particular, was renowned for its pearls.

The pearl mussel Margarithia Margaritifera (Cragen y Dulin) lives in clear, rapid, deep water and favours the soft waters of the mountain rivers. In 1856 the mussel could be found in the river Conwy from a mile upstream of Llanrwst bridge to Betws-y-coed, and in stretches of the river Llugwy. It was fished for from coracles on these waters.

The mussel was last found in 1955 but has not been observed since.

Whatever the quality of the pearls it would appear that they were fairly abundant in numbers; Spenser in his 'Faerie Queen' makes allusion to,

> "Conwy, which out of the stream doth send
> Plenty of pearls to decke his dames withall".

PENNANT, THOMAS

A leading 18th century zoologist and an ardent antiquarian, Pennant wrote four volumes of British Zoology in 1770, and his major work was the first comprehensive account of the fauna of the British Isles. His writings were not romantic like much of George Borrow, and as one would expect of a keen zoologist, his observations were more accurate.

Pennant's "Tours in Wales", published in 1778, provided considerable insight into the structure, life, culture and fauna of Wales, and enlightened the average Englishman (brought up on Dr Johnson), on the customs and character of the Prinicipality and its peoples.

He stayed in Betws-y-coed a year or so before publication of, "Tours in Wales", and devoted fifty pages in that book to the Snowdon area — indeed, some people claim Pennant was the originator of the title, 'Snowdonia'.

He considered that the noblest oak in all Wales grew on the western hillsides of the Conwy valley between Betws-y-coed and Gwydir Castle.

Thomas Pennant

Pennant showed more interest in the utilization of plants than in their biology, and while travelling somewhere in the uplands around Betws-y-coed, he noticed that the poor country people made a drink (Diodgrafol) by infusing the berries of the rowan tree in water. He also observed local people using the aromatic bog-myrtle leaves to keep their bedding fresh and for putting under beds to keep away moths and bugs. Bog-myrtle was also taken as a medicinal powder, and applied to the abdomen as a vermifuge.

Pennant described the presence of Razorbills, Guillemots, Gulls, Cormorants and Herons on the two Ormes at Llandudno, and his account of the locality is perhaps the first given by a naturalist.

In Llyn Conwy, Pennant describes, "three islands, one of which is the haunt of black-backed gulls during the breeding season. They are so fierce in defence of their young, that I knew of a man who was nearly drowned in an attempt to swim to the nests, being so violently beaten by the old birds".

PENTRE DU (Black Village)

The Betws-y-coed Council in 1899 went into the question of the status of the small hamlet of Pentre Du, situated on the western edge of the parish boundary, and always recognised as a part of the village. The hamlet consisted of 21 houses, and unless incorporated into the Urban District Council area it would not be connected to the water or sewerage mains.

A year later application for plans for a further 24 houses in Pentre Du to be built by Mr London of Hafodlas Quarry were submitted to the council for approval. They duly approved the plans when the Inspector confirmed that they were in accordance with the byelaws.

When the small community abandoned the upland hamlet at Rhiwddolion they moved down to Pentre Du, and the men found work in Hafodlas quarry or in the lead mines to the north of the village (See Miners' Bridge).

The new village school was opened here in 1928. The name Pentre Du is probably an allusion to the dark outlines of the slate quarry above, and the gloomy nature of the hillslope behind. The sun is hardly seen in Pentre Du between September and March and frost hardly clears there from one day to another in winter. On the other hand, the part of Betws-y-coed around the Waterloo Hotel is called Pentre Gwyn (White Village).

PESTILENCE

The disastrous outbreak of the Black Death in 1349 took a heavy toll of local residents and forced many to flee the district.

PETROL DRIVEN BUS

This vehicle first appeared in Betws-y-coed in 1911.

PLANTING RATES

In 1932 these were piece-work rates paid by the Forestry

Planting in the Gwydir Forest in the 1930's

Commission to all employees from Betws-y-coed and the surrounding district who were engaged in tree planting on the hillsides and uplands around the village. For every 1,000 trees planted the men were paid eight shillings and fourpence — or one old penny for every ten trees. When a man had planted 100 trees he could purchase two pints of ale and a box of matches for his tenpence.

PONT-Y-PAIR
(BRIDGE OF THE CAULDRON)

Haunt of almost every visitor to Betws-y-coed; photographed by many thousands; painted by several eminent artists, and beloved by those who just want to do what W. H. Davies exhorts us all to do, "A poor life this, if full of care, we have no time to stand and stare". And to just stand and stare is eminently satisfying.

Pont-y-pair was designed and partly built by Howell the

Pont-y-pair, Betws-y-coed

mason, of Bala, who died around 1475. By studying the design, shape and contour of the bridge, one can readily observe how the builder made maximum use of the natural rock formations available.

Upriver is Fir Tree Island, and between it and the bridge, Afon Llugwy cascades over the well-worn rocks in menacing vigour, yet, contrastingly, when viewed downriver, the Llugwy appears to have shed much of its energy and adopted a more leisurely progress. The pool here is quite deep in parts and attracts the local village lads, who demonstrate their diving skills by plunging into the waters off the rocks, and sometimes off the parapet of the bridge itself! To-day, Betws-y-coed is justly proud of its Pont-y-pair; in olden days this was the attractive feature around which the village grew.

Over many years during the latter quarter of last century and the early part of the nineteen-hundreds, a considerable amount of mining machinery, timber, roadstone and building materials had been carried across this bridge by horse-drawn waggons, and later by steam traction power.

It is a bridge for all tastes and seasons, and a location for everyone who admires the motion of water, has regard for an ancient structure and the spectacle of the stern backdrop of Clogwyn Cyrau.

PONT-Y-PAIR HOTEL

On the A5 just across from Pont-y-pair bridge.

The present hotel has been built on the site of the old "Swan Inn" by a Mrs Williams, whose husband invested a considerable sum of money in the development of Hafodlas Slate Quarry. He lost most of it within a short time, so they sold the hotel and emigrated to the USA. Subsequently a Mrs Brandreth (of Brandreth's Pills) lived there for some time before selling it to a brewery.

POOL MINE & BRIDGE

Not so very long ago there was another familiar bridge across Afon Llugwy. It spanned the river about a ½ mile downriver from Swallow Falls and remains are visible to-day. Evidence may be seen from the south bank of the Llugwy on Forest

Walk 4, and along another walk — to Swallow Falls — from the north side.

A large mill, constructed from sheets of corrugated zinc, stood on the south bank opposite to the bridge piers, and the bridge served the mill by having a tramway along which trucks brought out the ore from an adit 1400 yards long on the north side. Power used at the mill was obtained from water carried across the river in twelve-inch pipes to a pelton (turbine) wheel. Sections of these pipes may be seen to-day, and a leat that led the water to the first portion of piping can also be seen above Diosgydd Isaf.

The mill contained a stone breaker, a pair of rollers, two jigs, a record vanner and elevators, and the mineral, mostly lead, was then transported up a short length of track to the A5.

The adit at the north end of the bridge served also as a drainage level, and the ruins of a weighing shed can be seen near the entrance.

The mine appeared to be linked with Coedmawr Pool, and active intermittently between the late nineteenth century and 1927, when in March of that year, it closed. At the time eight men were employed below ground and six above. All the mill machinery was dismantled and taken away.

The bridge continued to serve the community — workmen crossed it going to Diosgydd nursery and occupants of the smallholdings used it on their way to catch buses on the A5. Nobody however seemed to be responsible for its upkeep, and in 1952 the bridge was declared unsafe and closed. During the ensuing years it quickly deteriorated. Sometime in the late 1970's the mill was taken down when many of the corrugated sheets were blown loose in a gale. Some 300 hundreds yards away, among the trees across the A5 from the mill, the explosive store still stands in good condition, the one substantial reminder of one of the parish's old abandoned lead mines.

POPULATION

Most of the 84 properties in 1800 were scattered among

woodland along the hillsides.

> In 1749 the population was 200
> In 1801 the population was 359
> In 1847 the population was 451
> In 1896 the population was 740
> In 1904 the population was 881
> In 1931 the population was 912
> In 1961 the population was 788
> In 1971 the population was 729

POSTWOMAN

While she lived, Miss Catherine Roberts, Postwoman, was one of Betws-y-coed's most durable and popular characters. In 1916 she had moved down from her home in Rhiwddolion, an upland hamlet above Betws-y-coed, to live with her brother and his family at No 8, Gethin Terrace, Pentre Du. Later she secured a post as postwoman, carrying mail to scattered outlying farms and smallholdings on the hillsides and moorland above the village.

Miss Robert's day began at 6am at the village post office and she set off on her rounds until the last mail was delivered sometime in the late morning. There might only be one letter or parcel on some days — to a lonely farm perhaps — but Catherine Roberts delivered it on a round that might involve her walking six or more miles. Her average daily walking mileage was between 8-9 miles and it was calculated that during all her days as postwoman she walked the equivalent of twice around the world.

Come storm of rain, wind or snow Catherine Roberts plodded on her rounds, seemingly as durable as the very crags she walked past on her way. Along narrow paths threading through heather, gorse and bilberry, across wet hollows covered in bog myrtle and through young plantations of spruce and larch, she carried the mail.

From Aberllyn to Pencraig, Penrallt to Glyn, day after day, year upon year, Catherine Roberts made her journey, and those visitors of to-day who might follow Forest Walk 6 (Plateau Walk) will pass through countryside that was very familiar to her.

At one period in her working life, when there was no mail to carry, she received no income. As soon as the forest smallholders became aware that a non-delivery day meant a loss of income for Catherine, they pledged to write and post letters to one another so that delivery was assured. Besides, their wives enjoyed a five minute chat with her so that they could catch up on all the local gossip and news!

Catherine Roberts retired in 1951, aged 60, and lived for a further 14 years in Pentre Du. Two nephews and a niece live there to-day, and in 1938 a reference to her career as postwoman was made in a local newspaper, with a picture of her in her uniform.

PURVEYORS OF MILK

In 1899 there were two purveyors of milk in the district — Ty'n-y-Bryn and Pen Clogwyn. The premises of each had been inspected and found in very good condition and the council confirmed that they be duly registered as Purveyors of milk.

Q

QUARTZ

While out on the hillsides and uplands, the walker will frequently come upon fragments of colourless and highly transparent crystals; sometimes they are variously tinted by impurities. They are crystals of quartz (Silicon Dioxide), the crystallised form of Silica, and are fairly common in the proximity of the lead mines to the north of the village.

As you walk along you may come across large pieces of quartz by the wayside, or often notice bands occurring separately in veins and crevices in rock faces. The crystals are frequently six-sided with pyramidal points, and are usually very hard.

Rarely one comes across a variety called rose quartz, which is a delicate shade of pink, and milky quartz, a white variety that owes its colour to the inclusion of very many air-filled holes. Small examples of quartz can be picked up by the side of paths or forest roads, but no one should venture near shafts or enter any levels to search for good specimens.

QUEEN OF SIAM

A distinguished visitor who stayed at one of the village hotels between the two World Wars.

QUERCUS (OAK) (DERWEN)

Of the two native oaks Quercus Petrea (Sessile Oak) is probably more suited to the soils of western Britain than Quercus Robur (Pendunculate Oak) and it is the Sessile oak that favours the Betws-y-coed district. However, the two kinds often hybridize and many intermediate forms occur. One of the features of the village are the well distributed oak trees growing along the main road.

The female flowers, and the resulting acorns of Sessile oak, are devoid of stalks and sit directly on the twigs. Its leaves however, are clearly stalked. Acorns are short, bluntly conical in outline and taper steadily from base to tip.

The early Council 'fathers' found too many trees, mostly oak, around the village. In the Council minutes of March 1899, the clerk was instructed to draw the Gwydir estate agent's attention to the Council's desire to thin out some trees about the village, and request the work be done before the onset of the tourist season.

How vexed and frustrated those poor council members must have been! The reply came from the agent on the 26th of January 1900, pointing out that he was giving his attention to having the trees thinned out within the village as requested! Not that nearly ten months growth would make much difference.

R

RAILWAY

Among such diverse world events in 1868 as Gladstone abolishing Church rates, Wilkie Collins completing "The Moonstone", and Wagner producing his "Die Meistersinger", the arrival of a rail link with Betws-y-coed from Llandudno Junction in that year might only appear significant to the local population. But one obvious advantage of the introduction of this railway would certainly be to swell the numbers of visitors to the village, and enable them to travel in comfort from the mainline along the North Wales coast. Furthermore, the journey would be speedier than by horse-drawn coach, and passengers would arrive far fresher and with less risk of suffering bruised and aching limbs.

Betws-y-coed had its railway and its terminus — a splendid railway station, built by that contractor of considerable talent — Owen Gethin Jones, creator of the imposing viaduct in the Lledr valley. The two-storied station had two platforms, a restaurant, a bookstall and offices. A covered footbridge led to the 'up' platform and goods yard.

In 1872, the London and North western Railway obtained Parliamentary powers to extend their line to Blaenau Ffestiniog, and work began a year later. Six tunnels were excavated, one being over two miles in length and taking five years to excavate. By 1879 the line was open for goods traffic only; it was two years before the first passenger train undertook the journey through the glorious Lledr valley.

Since 1968, Betws-y-coed station has been an unmanned halt. The footbridge remains, a little the worse for wear and somewhat neglected. But the entrance arch still evokes memories to those of us who recall the hordes of visitors passing beneath it during Wakes Weeks, and the evacuees from Liverpool streaming through from their trains.

Thousands upon thousands have come through that arch since Owen Gethin Jones erected it, and incorporated it with his splendid station — surely an enduring tribute to a man of such diverse talents as builder, poet and author.

RAILWAY LINE FIRE PATROLS

Part of the Betws-y-coed — Blaenau Ffestiniog railway line along the lower Lledr valley has quite a steep gradient. In the days of steam, the driver opened out the throttle while his fireman stoked away zealously on this particular section, producing dense volumes of smoke from the smokestack. While this was harmless enough in itself, the action also caused quantities of sparks to be emitted as well. These would alight in vegetation among the young plantations along the railway line and soon flare up and spread.

During hot weather forest employees were detailed to follow the 'up' trains as far as Gethin's bridge and extinguish any outbreak of fire with their beaters.

The first patrols were used in 1928 and continued for several years until the trees had grown tall enough to suppress any inflammable vegetation. Some replanting of those areas lost by fire went on for three to four years.

RHIWDDOLION (SLOPE OR HILL OF THE MEADOWS)

Tucked away in the gentle, part-wooded, part-pasture, countryside about a mile south of Miners' Bridge, the almost deserted upland hamlet of Rhiwddolion will be found. At an elevation of between 700-800 ft, and with its tumbling stream contributing significantly to this restful scene, the few fruit trees still evident in the old gardens, and the enclosed stone-walled pastures, are evocative of an age when the inhabitants of this hamlet sang their hearts out in song, and families came from isolated farms hereabout to Sunday service. There still exists to-day a well-defined flagged section of pathway leading to the chapel from opposite the entrance to Wyddfyd, and along this path over the years, several families must have travelled to and from Sunday worship.

Look at the simple names of the dwellings — Ty Uchaf (Highest house), Ty Isaf (Lowest house), Ty Mawr (Big house), Ty Newydd (New house) — all seem indicative of a close-knit, intimate community — which Rhiwddolion was.

Ruins at Rhiwddolion

This tiny, remote hamlet had its own shop at a time when nearly all the male members trod the lonely pathways across the hills to their place of work in the slate quarries, year in year out. A long-disused small quarry can be seen a little to the west, but most of the men trudged to Hafodlas Quarry close-by, or over to other quarries at Dolwyddelan or Penmachno.

A pathway along the course of a Roman Road (Sarn Helen) leading from the Lledr valley to Miners' bridge in the Llugwy valley, passes along the eastern edge of Rhiwddolion.

The hamlet's tiny chapel was built in 1869 and served a dual purpose — as a place of worship and a day school. The first headteacher was a G. H. Jones, more familiarly recognised by his Bardic name Gutyn Arfon, who composed the popular hymn tune "Llef" (beloved by all choirs and Welsh rugby supporters) here at Rhiwddolion, where he died in 1919.

G. H. Jones was a man of considerable energy — he founded a Betws-y-coed choral union, a brass band, a local opera company, several singing festivals and an annual eisteddfod which survived until hostilities began in 1939. He was instrumental in introducing a harmonium to the chapel, and this was in use right up until the chapel closed in 1956.

Boulder clay locally fills hollows about Rhiwddolion, and consists of grey to greyish-brown adhesive clay with, a high proportion of pebbles and boulders of local origin. From the point of view of topography, good hanging valley features from the south-west are well preserved here at Rhiwddolion.

As quarries in the locality closed, so the population dwindled and moved down to Pentre-Du in the valley. Rhiwddolion lost its last permanent inhabitant in 1974 — a man who had spent all his life there.

RHYS OF THE COCKS

One of the Forest Walks (No.2 Giant's Head Walk) leads the visitor close to an old farmstead called Mynydd Bychan (small mountain), where the remains of a small mansion once stood. Sometime around the year 1750 this place was inhabited by a miserly old bachelor named Rhys ab Hugh, better known as Rhys y Ceiliogod or Rhys of the Cocks — a man rebuked within the locality for his liking and support of that cruel pastime, cock fighting.

One night, he and his housekeeper spent a merry evening in a hostlery in Betws-y-coed, and it was very late as they ascended the path on their return homewards. (Their route can be followed behind St Mary's Church). When they reached a place where they could see their home in the distance they were confronted with the spectacle of the dwelling and outbuildings ablaze with fire and quite beyond saving.

Their grief was expressed in loud and prolonged lamentations and the site of these weepings and bewailings became known locally as Rhiwgri (Hill of Weeping).

Much later a smallholding called Rhiwgri was built on the spot and was last occupied by a forest worker named Ben Jones. (See under Jones, Ben).

Rhiwgri is now a ruin but can be seen at the side of a forest road leading to Llyn Elsi, and shown on a map in the official guide to Betws-y-coed.

A Telford milestone at Betws-y-coed

ROADS

During the 18th century, the Sovereign's messengers on their journeys to Ireland, passed through the Betws-y-coed district, and innkeepers, who were sparsely interspersed along the route, were paid twenty pence a day to maintain post horses. The hazards of the routes in those days could not be ignored: Thomas Pennant wrote in 1778 that the way through Llanberis Pass was a, "succession of rude and stony stairs" and the track through the Vale of Ogwen was, "the most dreadful horse-path in all of Wales".

However, these primitive communications and travels in the upper Conwy valley and in the mountain regions, were considerably eased by the construction of a road from Bangor to Betws-y-coed through the Nant Ffrancon Pass. The route took eleven years in the making and the first coach travelled along it in May 1795. At a period when the wars in France severed connection with the Continent for many visitors, opening up the beauties along this route more than compensated them for the loss of their haunts abroad. Thirteen years later the first Irish Mail coach passed through Betws-y-coed by crossing Beaver bridge, and in 1815 the road through the village had achieved the status of a main thoroughfare from London to Holyhead. Passenger fares at the time of the early Irish Mail runs from London to the Eagle and Child Inn in Holyhead, were six guineas (£6.30) for internal seating and ½ fare for those who favoured wind, rain and snow and huddled on outside seating!

In 1800, under the authority of an Act, the old packhorse track (now the B5106) between Betws-y-coed and Llanrwst via Gwydir Castle, was greatly improved. It was a Scots engineer (see Telford, Thomas), engaged by Parliament, who undertook the design for wholesale improvement to the London-Holyhead road.

In 1815 he began the creation of the modern A5 route; the highway would be nearly 260 miles in length and Betws-y-coed was the key to his plan of having no gradient steeper than 1 in 20. He by-passed Beaver bridge by constructing the cast-iron Waterloo bridge, and cut a new route across the steep features along Dinas hill, linking the bridge with Pentrefoelas.

An old Telford Tollgate, now seen at Coed Cynhelier

ROMAN REMAINS — CAER LLUGWY

The remains of this fort are located a little way west of the Betws-y-coed parish boundary, between Ty Hyll (Ugly House) and Capel Curig. The earthwork ramparts can be fairly well defined from the side road connecting the bridge at Ugly House and Pont Cyffyng.

Although not far outside the Betws-y-coed parish, there is a probable link with Sarn Helen (which comes down to the A5 at Miners' Bridge) and an old route through Maesnewyddion woods — where a pile of buried clinkers was discovered in 1938, indicating perhaps the site of a forge — continuing through Cae'n-y-coed fields and behind the Swallow Falls hotel to Craig Forys.

The Roman remains were traced in 1920 when excavation began. As the original roman name could not be found, it was given a new one Caer Llugwy (Llugwy fort). Many of the finds of the 1920-22 excavations are in the Museum of Welsh Archaeology in Bangor.

ROYAL OAK HOTEL

This imposing hotel is situated alongside the A5 in the centre of the village, and will always be associated with the artist, David Cox.

When he first came to Betws-y-coed, Cox stayed at the Royal Oak, which was then a small whitewashed inn. The artist found everything to his delight — glorious scenery to sketch by day and good food and cheerful company of an evening. He kept returning year by year, and in 1847 he painted the famous signboard which hung outside for many years.

When the present Royal Oak was built in 1861-62 the signboard was re-hung outside the new premises. In 1880 it was taken up to London and shown to the Court of Chancery who valued it at £1,000. It is now preserved in the hotel foyer.

During the heyday of the horse-drawn coaches, the hotel arranged visits to Beddgelert and Llanberis and retained its own coachmen.

Outside Royal Oak Stables c. 1890

In 1989 car parking space was extended, and across the A5, opposite to the hotel entrance, attractive formal prospects have been made at the approach by-road to the Visitor Information Centre, formerly the stables belonging to the hotel.

S

SAPPERS' (SUSPENSION) BRIDGE

Spanning Afon Conwy across from St Michael's Church, this bridge was erected in 1930 to replace an older wooden footbridge built by Royal Engineers between 1914-18 and which was swept away in a flood in 1928.

The placid stretch of river immediately downriver of this bridge is known as Church pool — on whose waters during late winter and springtime, the moorhen can often be observed making its way to a nest on a platform of aquatic vegetation in the bushes at the edge of the river.

By crossing the bridge from St Michael's side, and following a footpath, a point is reached at the side of the A470 from which a fine view across the village is obtained.

SCAVENGING

In view of the large number of horses employed by carriage owners and others in 1899, the need for daily removal of refuse during the summer months had become evident. This was particularly so at the entrance to the railway station where many residents had complained of the serious nuisance this caused.

The charge for carting refuse (manure) from the carriage stands was a shilling (5p) per hour. A Mrs Anne Evans undertook to do this and on an average summer's day she would receive 6 hours at 1/- (5p) – 6/- (30p). She then took the manure to the village rose-growers and made a shilling or two more!

SECULAR BUILDINGS

In a Conwy Valley Settlement Project in 1980, the object of a study carried out by students of Woolwich College was to map given data in a number of different settlements located mainly to the west of Afon Conwy. These settlements had been classified according to type and broad historical period.

Within the parish of Betws-y-coed the secular buildings investigated were:-
The Parish Church of St Michael.
An outbuilding with a roof of cruck form of the 17th century or earlier at Dolweunydd, Pentre Du.
Llanerch Elsi Cottage — 17th century.
Coedmawr Cottage — 17th century.
Mynydd Bychan Cottage — 17th century.
Iron Age stone fort (defended hilltop enclosure) at Tan Castell.
A 17th century unnamed cottage just south of Llyn Elsi. Ruins in a forest plantation.
Rhiwddolion cottages — 17th century.

SHEEP AT THE GATE

There were times in the 1930's when sheep strayed along the village streets and up the by-roads and paths leading into Gwydir forest. No one came forward to claim ownership of these sheep or felt any responsibility for their condition. They just roamed at will, chased out of gardens and churchyard, hotel grounds and station forecourt, their bodies clad in ragged shreds of wool from which any identifiable mark had long since disappeared.

And season after season the forest nurserymen contended with small groups of recalcitrant sheep who persistently outwitted their efforts to control them. What used to happen was this. Across the Diosgydd road (Llugwy Walk route), in those days, a gate had been erected to stop stray sheep from entering the nursery and young plantations adjacent to it, and it was always kept closed. The Diosgydd by-road appeared to be a popular place for these stray sheep despite the efforts of trappers to clear them out; some always eluded them and escaped into remote parts of the forest only to re-appear months later with their wool in tatters and spiked with bits of briar and gorse.

They clustered round the closed gate. While the nurserymen were at work they never had the opportunity to dive through it for they were chased down the road. The sheep grew wary. They remained at a discreet distance and watched and waited. They saw the men leave the nursery at the appointed hour, some on foot, others pedalling off on their bicycles. The last man closed the gate and made sure the latch was quite secure. The nursery and its immediate vicinity was deserted. The sheep waited awhile, then looked at one another as though quite re-assured. Their adversaries were out of the way for the day and the time was ripe to move forward to the gate; they ambled up and huddled as close as they could to it. If a local resident appeared they soon scattered out of the way and only re-mustered at the gate when that person had passed from their sight. They had, it seemed, the ability to recognise those who would not tolerate them close to this access point.

Presently, up the road, came a group of visitors on their way to Swallow Falls. They saw the sheep waiting at the gate in a compact little group, almost sitting up and begging to be let through, and showing no alarm whatsoever.

Inevitably it happened. With words of sympathy and tit-titting, the innocent visitors opened the gate and the eager sheep scampered through and in no time were in the nursery and among the young trees. This happened season after season.

It seemed as though the sheep were aware that, as soon as forest employees departed, strangers would presently appear and the gate would be opened for them. Instinct? Wisdom? Precognition? Sheep are frequently considered to be unpredictable, stupid and perverse, but by all accounts, the Diosgydd gate sheep deserve more credit than these attributes imply.

SMITHY

When one takes the by-road behind Spar Stores and follows it beyond the garage for a short distance, a modern bungalow will be seen on the right, a little way off the road. This overlooks the old Green Bank Smithy, active in 1803 when this road was the old turnpike route, before Telford's emergence altered its status completely.

In those far-off times farmers used to pay the blacksmith of the day with a sack of potatoes for a set of horseshoes.

ST MICHAEL'S CHURCH

This church, dedicated to St Michael and All Angels, is of 14th century origin and situated on the west bank of Afon Conwy between the river and the station. An earlier building very likely stood on the same site, as the bowl on the font appears to be a 13th century relic.

It is a small, dark church — unused to-day except for funerals — yet the imprint of local history is very much alive! Many tombstones date back to the late 17th century, and an 18th century stone pillar, which once supported a brass sundial, can be observed between the west end of the church and the west lych-gate, built in 1756. Alas! the sundial has not

St Michael's Church

been seen since 1966!

Oliver Cromwell was believed to have had an unwelcome relationship with this church, though not himself in person! A force belonging to Cromwell is said to have made its headquarters here during its stay in the neighbourhood, and aroused hostility among the village residents by plundering local cattle to provide food.

Traces of a fire could be seen within the church as late as 1843, when a large transept was added at the northern end and new windows were made in other walls. These alterations concealed the evidence of a fire, which probably dated back to Cromwell's troops' occupation.

A village day school came into existence in this church at the start of the 19th century, the first schoolteacher being the local saddler.

The wooden altar dates from around the late 17th century, and east and west windows contain some stained glass of the late 15th and early 16th centuries. Four old roof trusses remain, and a recumbent Knight's Effigy can be seen in the chancel. (See Effigy).

With the quiet flow of the Conwy the other side of a boundary wall, and the presence of its attendent yew trees, this old church adds dignity, grace and peace to its riverside position within the precincts of the village.

ST MARY'S CHURCH

Situated at the centre of Betws-y-coed, and with a backdrop of wooded hillside and imposing crags, services were first held in this beautiful church in 1873. It was built from the designs of Messrs Austin and Paley of Lancaster, and occupies the ancient site of a cockpit and fairground.

The style is close to early English and the lovely interior has a combination of various stone — the blue stone is local, the sandstone and floor tiles were quarried at Ancaster, and the font and sections of the pulpit comprise black serpentine from Cornwall. In 1929, the reredos — made of alabaster — was added.

The square tower has a chiming clock, introduced in 1907, and a peal of bells.

St Mary's Church

A spacious, well-illuminated church hall leads off from the front entrance. This addition to the church is commemorated by a stone with the following inscription:

This stone laid by
The Rt. Hon. Earl of Ancaster KCVO
On Sunday, 1st August 1976
In the presence of
The Most Reverend G. O. Williams,
Archbishop of Wales.

STILL POOL

This locally named stretch of Afon Llugwy is a short distance upriver from Fir Tree Island, and is one of the river's many attractions. As the name implies, it is a relatively calm surface of water at most times, extending to about a hundred yards in length, with a public footpath leading to Miners' Bridge along its north bank, and a picnic place close by.

A weir can be seen at the down river end to the pool, and at

Still Pool

one time just below this, a sluice gate was in position to control the volume of water leading into a leat which led to the Corn Mill's waterwheel. (See Mill Street).

SWALLOW FALLS (RHAEADR EWYNNOL)

This waterfall on the afon Llugwy has become a familiar natural celebrity over the past 100 years and has featured on film, postcard and canvas.

While its principal viewpoints are situated on the south bank of the Llugwy with the convenience of ample parking along the A5 and within the hotel car park, it is observed far more dramatically if approached on foot along the northern bank. Here, one follows a narrow, tortuous path — part hewed out of the rock face — with grey, fissured, threatening crags overhanging part of the route on the one hand and a forbidding abyss clothed with stunted trees on the other.

Swallow Falls from vantage point on the north bank.

Spectacular and dramatic, this approach path was at one time in the care of Betws-y-coed council workmen who took pride in maintaining its condition.

Unless there has been a heavy rainfall the summer months do not always present the viewer with the most exhilarating aspect of this famous waterfall — one needs a November or March flood when the water cascades over the dark, indented, weather-scarred rocks in a foaming, spewing onrush of unrestrained energy. But whatever the season, this waterfall will attract a world-wide selection of public to view it.

In 1913 the Swallow Falls was given to the Betws-y-coed council by the second Lord Ancaster. The council were more than pleased to accept it for they had incurred a debt of £15,000 through the installation of water and electricity supplies to the village, and it was anticipated that by charging to view the waterfall at close hand, it would provide a source of income to help pay off the debt.

Over the years it certainly did. Once the debt was cleared the parish retained the waterfall as a source of income until 1974 when Local Government Reorganisation reduced the status of the parish council. But what an interlude that proved to be! An interlude when Betws-y-coed was in the enviable position of being the only parish in Wales where its residents paid the lowest rates in the country!

T

TAN LAN (Below the church)

In a 1912 Guide book on Betws-y-coed, the advertisement under Tan-Lan claimed it was the largest and most modern Temperance Hotel in the village, and that tourists, cyclists and commercials would find every comfort.

A typical tariff for those days read:-
Plain Breakfast — 9p. With eggs — 1/-
Ham and eggs or chops — 1/6
Hot Dinners — 1/6 and 2/-
Teas from 8p

The advert in the Guide Book

Boarding from 30/- per week according to season.
Single room from 2/-
Rooms with two beds 3/- to 4/-
The proprietor was also agent for the White Star Line, Cunard Line, North Wales S.S.Co and G. W. Railway.

The property, situated in the centre of Betws-y-coed and opposite to the road leading to the station, was once kept by a Mrs Jones who, apart from bread, also sold bacon, pork, lard, flour and other commodities.

More recently, for many a year, Tan-Lan has belonged to the Parry family. It is popular as a coach stop and widely renowned for the quality of its bread and pastries, all baked and prepared on the premises by a member of the family.

Recent alterations have broadened the quality of service — there is choice of a self-service counter or waitress service.

Mountain bikes can be hired here and these are very popular. On by-road gradients in the neighbourhood, cycling is made to look very easy indeed by the users.

A variety of wines and spirits are available at the off-licence section in the shop.

THOMAS TELFORD (1757-1834)

In several ways, Thomas Telford, the brilliant Scots-born engineer, is synonymous with Betws-y-coed through one of his highway masterpieces — the Waterloo bridge. He was also responsible for the present-day Dinas Hill section of the A5, and it would seem a reasonable supposition to suggest he spent some time in the village while these operations were proceeding.

In 1811, Telford was commissioned by Parliament to survey the rebuilding of the highway from London to Holyhead, and by about 1830 he had completed this famous road and bridges across the Menai Straits and the mouth of the Conwy, masterpieces of engineering skill throughout.

Renowned for his skill in both architecture and engineering, Telford also operated his work contracts in a new way. He called for competitive tenders. In order to prevent engineers and contractors from arranging matters to their own benefit, Telford laid down strictly defined responsibilities for each. In this way he was ahead of his time.

In 1819, Parliament merged several small toll road authorities to form the Shrewsbury and Bangor Ferry Turnpike Trust, with Telford as their engineer, and nearly all the route from Betws-y-coed to Bangor was realigned.

Telford demanded high standards — from himself and his associates. His roadside toll houses have his special individual stamp of design, with their distinctive polygonal protrusion into the road so that the toll-keeper could observe both approaches. One of these tollhouses stood at the southern end of Pont-y-pair bridge.

His milestones were equally impressive, again with his own personal design. A cast-iron plate was sunk into a shaped block of stone with the appropriate mileage information carved on it — in those days miles, furlongs and yards. Such a milestone may be seen on the A5 opposite the entrance to Maesnewyddion woods and Llyn Elsi, and another faces the entrance to the school at Pentre Du.

Until about 1884, Telford's wrought-iron gates were in position alongside his toll-houses. The quality of design and structure are very evident — and one tollgate that has survived may be seen at the entrance to Coedcynhelier, about a ½ mile up the by-road from Pont-y-pair car park. It was once located at the junction of the A5 with Pont-y-pair bridge.

TERMINOLOGY

As Gwydir forest expanded some technical terms used to describe forest operations were introduced into the vocabulary of the parish. Wives of the smallholders would meet in shops, cafes and local markets and enquire of one another what their respective husbands were doing.

"Jack is brashing* by Llyn Parc".

"Will is beating-up* at Penrallt".

"Harry is lining-out* in Diosgydd nursery".

Brashing? Beating-up? Lining-out? Terms never heard of before in the language of the district.

"However that be, you'll doubtless agree
It signifies little to you or to me".

But by 1935, over ten years since the Forestry Commission's introduction to the locality, shopkeepers, tradespeople, postmen, hoteliers and council employees, among others, became familiar with the descriptions. The terms were soon being spoken about by the occupants of hotel bars; referred to among menfolk as they left chapel or church, voiced at local football matches and among the clamour of the local market. An outsider would have been forgiven for not caring to define them. (It reminded one of Dr Johnson, who, while compiling his dictionary, defined 'postern' as the knee of a horse. Asked by a kindly old lady how he came to do this he replied with admirable frankness, "Ignorance Madam, pure ignorance".)

The significant thing was that by the mid-1930's some phrases used in forestry had become firmly accepted locally.

* Brashing   Removing the dead lower conifer branches with a curved pruning saw to reduce fire risk and allow freer access into the interior of a plantation.

*Beating-up   Replacing trees which had succumbed in the initial planting.

Lining-out Nursery seedlings transplanted at the end of one or two years into beds with regular spacing between each plant.

An old photograph of Trawsafon

TRAWSAFON

Alas!, now in a ruinous state (Some Authority should set to and undertake some restoration work here!), this former cottage perches on the fringe of woodland behind St Mary's Church, and can be reached by a footpath leading off from the track up to Llyn Elsi. The junction of these paths meet some 200 yards up this track.

It was the home of a stonemason, Thomas Thomas, father of nine children, and its claim to a niche in local history rests in its being registered at the Bangor Diocesan offices as a Methodist preaching station in 1797 — the first official Non-Conformist meeting place in Betws-y-coed.

Eleven years passed, and the congregation grew all the while, so that in 1808 it was confident and active enough to obtain a lease on a site overlooking the main route through the village, and set to and build a chapel.

And to-day Bryn Mawr chapel stands proudly at the side of the road — the product of the dedicated members who gathered in a humble cottage named Trawsafon.

CAPTAIN TREHEARNE

Coed Derw (Oak Wood) is situated just off the B5106, a quarter mile north of Mill St.

It was built by a Captain Trehearne about 1879, and he imported timber from Norway for use in much of the interior work. The property was then let to Lady Alice Ewing, the fourth daughter of the Earl of Morten, and wife of the Rt Rev. Alexander Ewing DCL, Bishop of Argyll and the Isles. Subsequently it became the home of Mr Edward Buxton JP until his death, after which the property reverted to the Gwydir estate. During the second World War it was used as a hostel for ATS auxiliaries.

To-day it is the home of Mr and Mrs Evans, the owners of Anna Davies — a celebrated and popular shop situated next to the Royal Oak hotel.

TREWYDIR

Included in the minutes of Betws-y-coed's Urban District Council's meeting on January 28th, 1899, was a reference to consideration being given by the Council to what portion of the township of Trewydir should be included within the parish boundary.

It was agreed that the boundary should extend as far as Pont Sarn Ddu (and including the farm of Hafod Cae'n-y-Coed) and Rhiwddolion. The acreage involved would be about 1,000 and the rateable value some £450. The population was no more than 150 and no water or sewage works existed in Trewydir.

Furthermore, it was agreed that a notice of application be made to Caernarvonshire County Council (Now Gwynedd), asking them to issue an order to extend the Betws-y-coed area to embrace Trewydir.

Tref or Township, was not a cluster of houses grouped together, as the name might imply to a non-Welshman, but was simply a division of the countryside over which farms and tyddyns, and their lands, were scattered.

Tŷ Hyll

TŶ HYLL (UGLY HOUSE)

Not everybody would agree that this old structure should be
alluded to as ugly. Unique perhaps — or curious — but with a
charm of its own and located in a delightful setting.

Tŷ Hyll is slightly westward of the Betws-y-coed parish
boundary, being about ½ mile upriver of Swallow Falls and
close by the bridge carrying Telford's A5 across Afon Llugwy.
Telford completed his bridge here in 1821 and there was a
dwelling on the site of the present structure long before that
date — perhaps over 300 years before.

16th century Snowdonia was a wild and primitive
countryside and the fables of those times made reference to
any person who could construct some form of dwelling
overnight, and light a fire so that smoke could be seen coming
from the chimney by the break of dawn, could claim the land
freehold. Furthermore, he could extend the area of his
property as far as he could throw an axe from all corners of the
dwelling.

Perhaps Tŷ Hyll was a "Tŷ yn y Nos" (House of the night). Whatever its history it is a distinguished landmark along the A5 route between Betws-y-coed and Capel Curig, and is now in the care of the Snowdonia National Park Society who have diligently renovated the property as an 18th-19th century cottage.

TY'N-Y-BRYN

This property is reached by a short drive leading off from the Pont-y-pair car park.

It belonged at one time to the Gifford family who were related to Lord Penryn. Later it was occupied by a Doctor Fox, who practised in the village and was a local magistrate. Apart from medicine and the law, he was a very keen meteorologist and kept rainfall records and displayed large weather flags on a flagstaff at the rear of the house. These could be seen from nearly all quarters of the village.

When Dr Fox left, the house was bought by the Pullen family, then the owners of the Royal Oak hotel, and used by them as a private residence.

U

UPLANDS

From a selection of walks that convey the visitor through the upper hillsides, and finally on to the plateau land north and south of Betws-y-coed, it is possible to secure a picture of what living and working conditions were like in olden (and not so olden) times on these upland areas within the parish.

You can see the ruins of cottage smallholdings (tyddyns) and trace the outline of walled pastures; the occasional spring may be found, probably once, the only source of water for human and animal alike; the odd small mineral working can be seen, particularly in the mining region north of the village; and ancient tracks once trod by shepherds, quarrymen, gamekeepers and lead miners, lead the rambler back into the age of a lonely life, frugal living and a scarcity of proper communication. Carrying the weekly shopping and other essentials up those rough, stony tracks from the village to their dwelling on the uplands was hard going for any woman — and they were doing this up until the late 1930's, when the wives of forestry employees performed the task.

But long before this — though woodland covered the hillsides for centuries — tree vigour declined the higher one ascended, and much of the ground beneath the crags was occupied by scrub growth of oak, birch, hazel and hawthorn. The ground was rock-strewn in a series of broken terraces; the soils were thin; and exposure to the prevailing westerlies was frequently severe.

Yet, several cottage smallholdings (tyddyns) were built among the woods, often nestling beneath a rocky background for shelter. Patches of scrub were cleared for cultivation wherever possible and stock were allowed to graze in the more open spaces. Life in these tyddyns in the 18th and much of the 19th centuries was hard and provident — there were no luxuries and little time for relaxation. Comfort was homespun — a few wooden chairs, a long table, a high-backed settle, and a two-piece cupboard (Cwpwrdd Deuddarn). The beds were filled with soft hay and the woollen homespun clothing was coloured with vegetable dyes made from lichens collected off the rocks.

The undulating plateau land, between 500-700 ft above Betws-y-coed, comprises a series of fractured ridges of uneven height, dense heather banks, scattered conifer plantations, pockets of scrub woodland and an occasional lake. It extends to the foothill country surrounding the principal massifs east of Moel Siabod, the Snowdon group and the Carneddau, and due to the broken character of this countryside, any land cultivation within it has always been limited to a low percentage of its total area. For centuries, parts of these uplands provided summer grazing for stock brought up from lowland farms (See Hafod and Hendre).

The Acts of Enclosure ensured that better land was enclosed by stone walls and the upland mountain pasture became separated from the lowland farms; the summer migration had ceased by around 1860 and sheep farming became prevalent in the hill farming economy.

Occupants of the smallholdings on these uplands above the village were hard put to it to survive on stock-tending alone, and finally, the head of the household could no longer support a family, and became more and more dependent on any alternative employment he could secure. This usually meant the unhealthy atmosphere of the local lead mines and quarries, and when, eventually, all these work outlets closed down due to economic stringency, there was extreme hardship for the tyddyn dwellers. Gradually they were forced to give up an unequal struggle and abandon their smallholdings on the uplands; some migrated to America, others found work in the mills and factories in Lancashire.

The tyddyns stood vacant and forlorn, symbols of a bygone age.

> "All within is dark as night,
> In the window is no light,
> And no murmur at the door,
> So frequent on its hinge before".

A chapter in the history of the uplands of Betws-y-coed parish has long closed. Some of its past may be observed on several of the advertised walks from the village, and the visitor will soon be aware by the very nature of the terrain he travels through, of the wearying conditions of life the smallholders endured.

URBAN DISTRICT COUNCIL

What a distinction! What exceptional circumstances! — to have been for long the smallest Urban District in the country in terms of population.

Its first councillors, nine of them, were elected in 1898, to serve an area of over three-and-a-half-thousand acres, containing some seven hundred head of population. Shortly the number of elected members rose to eleven, and the premises they held meetings in were in the old courthouse (now Henllys private hotel), near St Michael's Church. Twenty-nine years later they occupied a small chamber in what is now a climbing equipment and sports shop opposite Pont-y-pair bridge.

The council employed a clerk (See Nineteen-Hundred),

and their very first purchase was a Gladstone bag to contain his papers. They haggled over gas supplies until they eventually approved of gas lighting, before electricity came in 1913 when the Council introduced a new mains water supply from Llyn Elsi, where the lake was linked to a hydro-electric generator.

The 1899 Council members introduced some fire hose and a handcart to carry it; thus a Betws-y-coed Fire Brigade came into existence, and the equipment remained unchanged for about forty years, until, during the early years of World War two, the Government set up a unit of the Auxiliary Fire Service in the village, when a trailer pump and towing van made their appearance.

Inevitably, though sadly — when one respects the history of the Urban District Council and its long term of stability — events brought about change, and under the 1974 re-organisation of Local Government, the Betws-y-coed Urban District Council ceased to exist as an independent body. The village is now administered as part of Aberconwy District Council.

But what a final gesture the old Council made! What a triumphant departure from stewardship! They decided unanimously to abolish their rate for their final year of independence! Considering that at 4p in the £ the previous year their rate was already the lowest in the country!

V

VIEWPOINTS

On some walks from the village a number of viewpoints are either mentioned in the guide book text or indicated on diagrams. However, not all can be clearly indentified on the ground, and interprative panoramic illustrations at some given points would be of advantage to a visitor.

Fortunately, as one emerges from the valley confines and sets out across the plateaux, several natural viewpoints offer spectacular panoramas of distant mountain ranges (Arenigs), closer peaks such as Moel Siabod, Tryfan, and profiles of the

Snowdon group, much spectacular foothill country, mixed woodland, open spaces, crags, gullies and a rich assortment of colour, shades and vegetation texture.

There is a rich fabric of landscape scenery to observe whichever walk one decides to follow. Perhaps the plateau north of the village provides a wider variety of perspectives — there are old mineral workings to observe, more lakes to sit by, wider views to the east across the Conwy valley, and a few well-sited picnic places (themselves good viewpoints) affording broad scenic prospects.

Not to be outdone though, uplands south of Betws-y-coed contain Llyn Elsi, surely a scenic jewel, and on some of the walks there are good views overlooking the Lledr valley. Then there is the tranquil old hamlet of Rhiwddolion to observe, and the Roman route (Sarn Helen) to walk along. Fine views of Moel Siabod and Glyders are clearly defined to the south-west.

VILLAGE EDUCATION

During 1749 seventeen school sessions were held over a three month period to instruct children during the day, and older people of an evening, to read the Bible. A total of 751 pupils were instructed that year.

(From Welch Piety, 1755-57)   Betws-y-coed, May 13th, 1757

'This is to certify that R-------M-------, Master of the Welch Charity School in this parish, hath behaved himself in a careful and diligent manner, the children under his care daily improving in their reading and catechism. Though the poverty of their parents and the scarcity of corn in these parts, have lessened his daily numbers by their being obliged to beg from door to door most of the time. For this reason, the parishioners and myself humbly beg you to be so good as to leave him with us for another quarter, as he is so beneficial to the poor people. And may the blessing of Almighty God accompany this work of charity, which He has put into the hearts of his servants on behalf of these poor children. That being trained up in the way they should go, when they are old, they may not depart from it. May He of his mercy, keep them safe amidst the dangers of this bad world through which they are to pass, and preserve them into Heavenly Kingdom, is the sincere prayer of . . .etc. . .

William Evans,
Curate Ibidem.

VILLAGE TOURIST FACILITIES

Betws-y-coed offers an abundant choice of facilities for the visitor. The village's reputation for accommodation, catering and hospitality — gained a century and more ago — remains well in evidence to-day. Local places of attraction and beauty retain the distinction given them by Victorian artists and writers; the backcloth to the village maintains its craggy, wooded character.

What has changed is the variety and quality of available resources. For the visitors who prefer to dawdle leisurely through the village, browse among its diversity of shops, and contemplate the capricious progress of the Llugwy or the smoother flow of the Conwy, there is a great deal to claim their attention and appreciation.

For those who prefer to be more actively engaged — and to forego the animated scene of traffic moving along the crowded roads for a few hours — encouragement to explore and enjoy the peace of the surrounding countryside and woods is provided by a series of waymarked routes starting from the village. These lead the rambler through a wide diversity of scenic habitats, and many relics of a past way of life may be observed.

FACILITY	REMARKS
Visitor Information & Interprative Centre	Provides much local Advice. Selection of books, leaflets etc. Farm and Forest section. Interprative maps of Snowdonia. Fishing. Evening talks are occasionally held.

Conwy Valley Railway Museum	History of the local railway line. Artefacts & railway memorabilia. Rides on narrow-gauge circuit. Restaurant coach serving light meals.
9-Hole Golf Course	Just beyond St Michael's Church. Splendid situation between the river Llugwy & Conwy. Clubhouse. All visitors welcome.
Caravan & Camping	Adjacent to Golf Course, in pleasant central situation.
Hotels	Six in number, all situated on the south side of the A5. Most with traditions of a long association with local history.
Guest Houses	All well appointed and pleasantly situated. Many with long standing reputations for excellent service.
Restaurants	All centrally placed. Catering and service widely approved.
Angling	River and lake fishing available. Details at Information Centre and Gwydir Hotel.
Craft & Souvenir Shops	All centrally placed. Presenting a wide range of quality articles & gifts. Guidebooks and leaflets available at most shops.
Public & Forest Waymarked Routes	Routes take the visitor deep into Gwydir forest; many offer splendid panoramic views of the Snowdonia mountains and upland lakes.
Cae Llan	The "Village Green" — in the centre of the village between St Mary's Church and the Visitor Centre. An open space to relax in. Seating. Toilets close by. Freedom for children to play.

Concerts & Films	Sometimes held in the Memorial Hall. Details will be announced at many places in the village.
Guided Walks	Usually half-day interprative excursions starting from the Information Centre. Details available there.
Post Office	One of the village's pride of place. A recent award-winner for decor and elegance.
Sherpa Bus	A service provided to take the visitor to a selection of places within Snowdonia. Buses stop and return at various times.
Motor Museum	A collection of vintage or post-vintage cars.

PLACES OF NATURAL BEAUTY

Pont-y-pair, Fir Tree Island, Still Pool	Historic bridge and river scenes.
Swallow Falls	Widely famous falls on the Llugwy.
Fairy Glen	Within about a ½ mile walk from the centre of the village.
Miners' Bridge	Reached by a pleasant walk along the banks of the Llugwy.
Meeting of the Waters	Meeting of the Conwy and Llugwy rivers in a pastoral setting just north of the Golf Course.
Clogwyn Cyrau	Picturesque Crag overlooking the village to the north. Reached by public footpath.
Various Lakes	Lakes Elsi, Parc, Geirionydd, Bodgynydd, Crafnant, and some smaller shallow lakes created during the heyday of the mineral workings north of Betws-y-coed.

VIVIPAROUS LIZARD

This little reptile is quite common in the locality, being a familiar sight basking in the sunshine on mossy banks, walls and rocks. It is an agile little creature, but when it can be caught by its tail it can break this off and make its escape without it, subsequently growing a new one from the stump and suffering no ill effects.

W

WAKES WEEK

Every Whitsun and August Bank Holiday during the 1930's the excursion trains steamed into Betws-y-coed station releasing hundreds of cheerful, excited Lancastrians on a day's outing during their Wakes Week holiday from the mills and factories of Accrington and Ramsbottom, Darwen and Oswaldtwistle.

They stayed at resorts along the N. Wales coast, but for one day they were the guests of Betws-y-coed and they were among the jolliest and best behaved visitors the village residents had ever experienced. For their part the "lads and lassies from Lankysheer" were convinced there was no more delightful place in the country than Betws-y-coed. Their association with the village became a very special one.

The first arrivals came in at 9.30am and the last train returned them to their resorts about 8.30 in the evening. The rival village taxi-owners glowered at one another as they whisked folk off to Fairy Glen or Swallow Falls — friends for fifty-one weeks of the year, the arrival of Wakes Week appeared to bring about a complete metamorphosis of character, as though they were suddenly overcome with mistrust and intolerance toward one another. From what one heard at the time half the good folk who paid to be conveyed to Swallow Falls were dropped off half-way at Miners' Bridge and told that if they walked upriver they'd be at the Falls in a few minutes — "You'll see two spots of local beauty for the price of one", a taxiowner informed his suspicious passengers.

Most of them walked though — to Llyn Elsi, Llyn Parc, Swallow Falls, Beaver Pool and took their tea in Tan Lan cafe, Station cafe, Llugwy tea rooms and Oakfield. They talked cricket to forest nurserymen who were having their lunch break at the side of Diosgydd road, and many returned year after year to renew acquaintanship with the foresters. Addresses were exchanged and right up to the outbreak of War in 1939 Christmas cards were delivered to Penrallt and Allt Isaf from Mabel and Bill from Darwen or Sally and Arthur from Ramsbottom.

At Whitsun 1937 a party of visitors from Accrington helped put out a plantation fire on the way to Llyn Elsi, and two years later another group from Lancashire accompanied Dr Bowden from Betws-y-coed and four foresters who went to the aid of a youth who had fallen down the steep slope downriver from Swallow Falls and broken a leg. Under the doctor's direction the party helped haul the youth up the slope on a makeshift stretcher to a waiting ambulance outside the Swallow Falls hotel.

On a late August Bank Holiday evening in 1939 a tired but cheerful throng gathered on the platform at Betws-y-coed station, awaiting the last of the Wakes Week excursion trains to arrive. It was a month of national crisis and there were many in that group who would not visit the village again.

The stationmaster listened to renderings of popular tunes of the 1930's — "Bicycle made for Two", "Red Sails in the Sunset", "Isle of Capri" and "She's a Lassie from Lankysheer", and like the two porters and the ticket collector, he couldn't resist joining in the several choruses with enthusiasm. The train pulled in and the crowd entered their compartments and the doors slammed shut. People leaned out of the windows and waved and shouted, 'Good luck', and they were still waving as the train passed from sight of the station, leaving behind an empty platform, a subdued station staff, and the quiet village which they'd had a very close and special relationship with over many an annual Wakes Week visit.

WATERING CART

In 1899 the Council agreed that the village streets should be watered during summer months when their dusty condition in dry weather became an annoyance.

The only watering cart available was owned by the Waterloo hotel, and the Council offered to purchase it. However the proprietress, Mrs Mc Culloch, would not sell it, but was prepared to loan it to them free of charge for the summer months.

A typical charge for watering was 7½ days @ 8/-(40p) - £3.0.0.

WATERLOO BRIDGE

A Telford masterpiece carrying the A5 across Afon Conwy, and the seventh bridge ever built to be constructed of iron.

Erected in 1815, and so named after the decisive battle fought in Belgium that year, this landmark in bridge

The Waterloo Bridge

construction was known locally as Y Bont Haearn (The Iron Bridge).

The span is 105 feet and the pierced spandrels are splendidly decorated with the leek, rose, shamrock and thistle — emblems of Wales, England, Ireland and Scotland. Prominently inscribed in cast iron and covering the full length of the span on both sides are the words "This arch was constructed in the same year the battle of Waterloo was fought."

A few years ago the bridge underwent a complete structural overhaul. The days of the horse-drawn coaches carrying the Irish mails, with the accompanying blare from the guard's posthorn echoing across the valley, may be long gone, but this structure still remains as it was then — and capable of sustaining the daily weight and burden of scores of heavy lorries, and coaches, and the ceaseless flow of lighter traffic using the A5 route.

WATERLOO HOTEL

A coaching advertisement for 1883 proclaims: "On and after Whit Monday, the 14th of May 1883, the proprietor of the Waterloo Hotel will run his well appointed four-horse coach 'Enterprise' daily from Betws-y-coed to Llanberis and back. Passengers wishing to proceed to Beddgelert will be forwarded by the proprietor of the hotel at Pen-y-gwryd. Seats can be booked at the Waterloo Hotel. The coach leaves the hotel about 9am and will await the arrival of the 9.13am train from Llandudno Junction at the end of the station road".

L. B. McCulloch, Proprietor.

A further advertisement for that year declares: "Waterloo Hotel, Betws-y-coed. Close to Waterloo bridge and a few minutes walk from the railway station. Standing in its own grounds. Handsome and well-appointed and ventilated Billiard and Smoke rooms. Excellent stabling and lock-up coach house. Posting in all its branches. Large lawn tennis grounds. A well appointed omnibus attends all trains."

L. B. McCulloch, Proprietor.

The McCullochs appear to have had a long association with the Waterloo Hotel, for in a 1912 brochure (29 years later) the only difference in title is:-

Mrs McCulloch, Proprietress.

So much for the massive, distinctive, old Victorian coaching hotel in its spacious grounds and its attendant grooms, coachmen and hall porters. During the 1939-45 war it was requisitioned as a hospital for wounded military personnel.

Except in photographs and paintings no evidence of the old building remains to-day. Its replacement is a splendid, functional hotel and motel, with modern comforts and facilities offered to the visitor.

In 1989, 16 new suites were made available and 4 self-catering cottages — all prudently located in the grounds behind the hotel.

But the highlight of 1989 development must be the addition of a spacious leisure and fitness centre with a range of Club Membership Categories for the use of the following — heated swimming pool, jacuzzi, children's splash pool, sauna, solarium, steam room, four station multigym, two quality exercise bikes, and a treadmill.

All these facilities are free to members, and categories include Family membership, Corporate membership and "Young at Heart" for senior citizens. One wonders just what the McCullochs would say to all this!

WILL HERB AND HIS LANTERN TREE

There is a venerable oak tree growing alongside the Diosgydd road near the remains of Pool Mine bridge, some ½ mile downstream from Swallow Falls. You will see this tree if you follow the Llugwy Gorge Walk (Forest Walk 5) — locally, in the 1930's, this oak was alluded to as Will Herb's lantern tree.

Will Herb was a local character who drifted from farm to farm doing odd jobs. Finally he became domiciled with his few personal belongings in a draughty outbuilding on an upland farm above Diosgydd nursery, and continued performing chores such as helping out at sheep shearing time, haymaking, digging ditches, repairing stone walls and chopping firewood.

Will Herb was middle-aged, lean of frame and feature and always wore a soiled checked cap pulled well over one ear, and a polka-dotted cravat knotted round his neck. He kept himself clean and tidy always.

He got one square meal a day from the farmer who permitted him use of his outbuilding and a few shillings for odd jobs around the farm; other than that he subsisted on what he bought himself or what other people offered him in return for chopping logs or cleaning ditches. Without doubt Will Herb lived frugally, but he remained healthy and active and never appeared downcast.

Once a week he spent an evening at the Swallow Falls hotel. To get there he followed a miners' track leading downhill below the ancient oak tree, crossed Pool Mine bridge (now only the remains of two piers exist), and joined the A5 a few hundred yards from the hotel.

These once-weekly excursions were late sittings for Will Herb and he often left the hotel in a befuddled state, arriving at Pool Mine bridge on wobbly limbs and clinging despairingly to the wire handrails as he crossed over. On dark evenings he found difficulty in detecting the path leading up to the oak tree beside the Diosgydd road, and he frequently sprawled down the hillslope and into the pools on the banks of Afon Llugwy.

A beacon was the only answer he finally decided. He procured a lantern (he was never known to possess a torch) and when he got to the oak tree on his outward journey to the hotel, he lit it and hung it on one of the branches. And there was the re-assuring glow, and Will descended the path full of confidence.

But his scheme never really functioned efficiently. Sometimes he was too befuddled to look in the right direction; at other times the lantern went out or was swung off the branch by the wind. And it was not past one or another of the local smallholders, aware of his habits, to mischievously remove the lantern, turn it out, and leave it at the foot of the tree.

Will Herb endured countless tumbles on his way up the path below this tree and the experiences rarely sobered him up completely. The oak tree was always his objective; once he arrived at its side he somehow managed to manipulate his passage on up through Diosgydd nursery to his draughty outbuilding.

Few to-day can recall his contests with this hillside or his trust in the lantern. But the oak tree still stands — a landmark in the exploits of an amiable, if wayward, local character.

X

XYLOTA SEGNIS (HOVER FLY)

This member of the hoverfly fraternity is probably one of the commonest come across in the parish. It is between 10-13mm in length and is seen in woods and scrub, and on rocks warmed by summer sunshine. When it alights on leaves, it scurries back and forth and consumes the honeydew from any aphids it finds.

When basking, with its wings folded over the abdomen, it could readily be mistaken for a wasp. The larva lives in rotten tree stumps.

When more than one hover fly settle close to one another, they emit a familiar high-pitched 'whine' and every few minutes make darting sallies at each other. This hoverfly is usually silent when alone, and first settles on a surface, and then when the wings close tightly, the 'whining' begins — just as though the very movement switches on the sound.

Y

YELLOWHAMMER

During the 1930's and the following two decades or so, this delightful little bird with its yellow and brown plumage, became rare within the parish.

However, to-day it is fairly well distributed and may be seen or heard on several walking routes that take the visitor through areas where young undergrowth is prevalent. The yellowhammer is closely associated with gorse during the breeding season, particularly on scattered clumps over rough ground. It frequently nests within the gorse cover. Typical habitats can be seen along Walks 4 and 9 in the official Guide to Betws-y-coed, and along Walk 6 of 'Walks in Gwydir Forest'.

The Yellowhammer breeds between May and June normally and between 3 and 5 eggs are laid. These are white, sometimes with just a touch of pinkish flush, and irregular mauve scribbles across the shell.

The song is a popular one, described best as, "little bit of bread and no cheese", and may be heard from as early as late February.

The Yellowhammer is also known as the Yellow Bunting.

YEWS

In St Michael's Churchyard there are three very ancient Yew trees planted in a row (a few younger trees may be observed too). These three Yews are of unknown age, but recalling the antiquity of this venerable church, they have survived six centuries and probably longer.

The Yew is native to the United Kingdom, and is commonly planted in churchyards because, as it is an evergreen, it is a symbol of immortality. Furthermore, the association of this tree dates back to early Christian times, and it was planted by Druids near their temples.

Female flowers of the Yew ripen by October to crimson berries, each containing a seed within a cup. Birds eat the berries and void the seeds. Yew clippings, bark and seeds are poisonous to livestock, though animals rarely suffer harm from nibbling growing foliage.

Pollarded Yew tree branches were used to make longbows, and Welsh archers, in particular, were renowned for the accuracy and speed of their archery. At the battles of Crecy (1346) and Agincourt (1415), it was the contribution made by Welsh archers that influenced the victorious outcome.

Their six-foot long bows propelled an arrow up to twenty-seven inches long with an effective range of almost 240 yards and a maximum range of 340 yards. Six shots a minute could be discharged. In 1351 each arrow cost 1½ pence and in 1462 arrow heads were five a penny.

Z

ZINC

This was the principal mineral mined for at Aberllyn mine between 1869-1904, when some 2,548 tons of zinc ore were raised (See under Aberllyn Mine).

During its active working life this mine employed more workmen than any other mine within the parish.

In nature, zinc usually occurs with lead, though they are very different in their chemical and physical properties.

Galvanising accounts for about 40% of the zinc product.

SELECTED MILESTONES IN THE HISTORY OF BETWS-Y-COED

1349   Outbreak of the pestilence (Black Death) took a heavy toll of the lives of local residents and forced many to flee the district.

1468   Lledr bridge built.
Betws-y-coed and the surrounding district laid waste by an army led by the Earl of Pembroke during the Wars of the Roses.

1536   Betws-y-coed comprised one of five parishes within the Nant Conwy Hundreds.

1749   The population of the village was 200.

1797   The village dwelling known as Trawsafon was registered as a Methodist preaching station.

1801   Betws-y-coed was a parish of 85 houses.

1803   The first four-wheeled carriage crossed Beaver bridge.

1808	The first Irish Mail stagecoach passed through the village.
1815	Waterloo bridge was built to Thomas Telford's design.
1847	David Cox, the celebrated artist who favoured Betws-y-coed above all other places, painted the famous 'Royal Oak' signboard.
1850	First exploratory work at Aberllyn lead and zinc mine.
1866	The first Police Sergeant appointed to the village.
1868	The railway reaches Betws-y-coed from Llandudno Junction, increasing the status of the village as a holiday resort.
1869	Opening of the first purpose-built school in the village.
1873	The first service is held in St Mary's Church.
1879	The railway line is extended from Betws-y-coed to Blaenau Ffestiniog for the conveyance of goods. Two years later it was open to passenger traffic.
1884	There were six licensed hotels, five temperance hotels and thirty-four boarding houses in the village.
1898	The first meeting of Betws-y-coed Urban District Council — for a long time thereafter the smallest UDC in the country in terms of population.
1899	The first two Purveyors of milk were registered within the parish.
1906	Betws-y-coed's first garage opened.
1911	The first petrol-driven bus made its appearance in the village.
1913	Electrically-lit street lighting was introduced. Prior to this date, gaslit street lighting (via a local gasworks) had been in service since 1899.
1920	Spring-running fish first introduced in a hatchery on the river Lledr by the owner of the Gwydyr hotel.
1921	Replanting began on the hillsides around Betws-y-coed by the Forestry Commission to restore timber lost by wholesale felling during the 1914-18 hostilities.
1930	The Suspension bridge (Sappers' bridge) near St Michael's Church was erected.

1938	In May of this year the largest fire in Gwydir forest burnt 411 acres of plantations around Parc lake.
1940	The last year that the Corn Mill in Mill Street was in operation. Dulwich College Prep School evacuated to Betws-y-coed and based at the Royal Oak hotel.
1947	Prolonged and very severe winter weather.
1948	Diosgydd forest nursery, near the Swallow Falls, closed. Over 16,000,000 young trees had been raised there since 1925 for planting in local and distant forests.
1951	Postwoman Catherine Roberts retired. It was calculated that during her years of service she had walked the equivalent of twice around the world.
1955	The last pearl mussel claimed to have been found in the river Conwy.
1961	Population of the village was 788.
1963	Ice flows seen in the river Conwy for the first time in living memory.
1971	The village population was 729.
1974	Conwy Valley Railway Museum opened.
1976	Garth Falls Walk for the elderly and handicapped was opened.
1977	Betws-y-coed Golf Club opened.
1981	The Visitor Information Centre opened on the site of the former stables and courtyard belonging to the Royal Oak hotel.
1985	The Motor Museum opened where the Royal Oak farm buildings were once located.
1988	The year when Mountain Bikes were introduced to the village and could be hired from Beics Betws, Tan-Lan. An Award for Betws-y-coed Post Office — 1st Runners-up Prize for the Wales and Marches Brightest and Best Kept Sub-Post Office Competition.
1989	The Dukes Leisure and Fitness Centre at the Waterloo Hotel was opened.